A. Patchett Martin

Australia and the Empire

A. Patchett Martin

Australia and the Empire

ISBN/EAN: 9783743306868

Manufactured in Europe, USA, Canada, Australia, Japa

Cover: Foto ©ninafisch / pixelio.de

Manufactured and distributed by brebook publishing software (www.brebook.com)

A. Patchett Martin

Australia and the Empire

AUSTRALIA

AND

THE EMPIRE

BY

A. PATCHETT MARTIN, F.R.G.S.

EDINBURGH: DAVID DOUGLAS

1889

[*All rights reserved.*]

TO THE

RIGHT HON. ARTHUR JAMES BALFOUR, M.P.

This Volume is Dedicated

AS A SLIGHT MARK OF THE PUBLIC APPRECIATION

AND

PERSONAL ESTEEM IN WHICH HE IS HELD

BY ALL CLASSES

OF HER MAJESTY'S LOYAL SUBJECTS IN THE COLONIES.

PREFACE

In submitting this little sheaf of Essays to the British public, as a slender contribution to the great Imperial discussions of the day, I have only to express my regret as a loyal colonist that I cannot support the policy enunciated by that respectable section who are known as Imperial Federationists. With the object of their League, and particularly with the aims of its late lamented Chief, William Edward Forster, I feel the greatest sympathy; but the means suggested, and the policy formulated, seem to me the reverse of wisely constructive. Certainly, unless the whole character of our Parliamentary Government undergoes a radical change, a common Imperial Assembly, meeting at Westminster—or elsewhere—would simply be a cumbrous and unwieldy engine, only capable of bursting and blowing its engineers into fragments.

The opening political sketch of Lord Sherbrooke

in Sydney has been compiled largely from information and printed papers supplied to the author by that distinguished statesman. It has purposely been made short and sketchy, but will, I trust, be read with some interest in Australia, where Robert Lowe, though bearing an honoured name, has by no means as yet received the full measure of recognition due to his services for the commonweal.

Chapters III. and V. originally appeared in a briefer form, as two articles by a "Colonial Contributor" in the *Morning Post*. I can only hope that the additions made to them for the purposes of this book will not lessen the good opinion which some influential persons were kind enough to express of them in their original shape.

With regard to Chapter VIII., I would say here that it would not have appeared in this volume save for the recent upheaval of a class of publications about the colonies, of which Mr. Hogan's *Irish in Australia*, and Sir C. Gavan Duffy's magazine essays, are the most typical specimens. If my readers will turn to these effusions, they will not fail to recognise that however outspoken I may be in expressing my opinions on the subjects in dispute, I at least am not the aggressor. Referring to the two gentlemen I have named, let me also add, that however much one may dissent from their sentiments and views, it is idle to deny that they both have what we Australians particularly prize, as "colonial experience"—which in one case is turned to the best account by considerable literary skill. From a careful perusal of these writings, I have come to the conclusion that their chief aim is to show, by the successful working of responsible government in Australia, that Englishmen should advocate the policy known as "Home Rule" for Ireland. I have attempted to prove that there is no analogy between the two cases. If, moreover, it be considered laudable for colonial Irishmen to write the history of Australia from a purely Irish standpoint, surely a colonial Englishman may be permitted to tell the same story in his own fashion. I am thus frank in avowing the controversial, but I trust not bitter or unfair, spirit of this section of my book. Personally I would have preferred to give my views and opinions on *Australia and the Empire* free from the fray of party polemics. My book was, in fact, almost finished when I became acquainted with the recent writings of these Irish-Australian annalists. Nor would I have deemed their views of any significance as bearing on my subject, but for the mysterious "conversion" of Mr. Gladstone to the principles, if not the practices, known as "Parnellism," which are in my judgment fatal to the continuance of the British Empire. The effect of Mr. Gladstone's Irish Home Rule Bill on the Australian public mind is best typified by the contrast between Mr. David Gaunson, then the leading Native Victorian politician, speaking eloquently on behalf of the "Australian Natives' Association," in support of Mr. Service and Mr. Francis, on the occasion of the great Beaconsfield demonstration, at the Melbourne Town Hall, on July 29th, 1878 (see page 69), and the "base uses" to which, according to Mr. Gowen Evans (see page 250), these "Australian Natives' Associations" are everywhere being turned since the "conversion" of Mr. Gladstone, and the surrender of so large a section of his party, to the policy of disintegration.

It is lamentable, but very natural; for—as Sir Samuel Griffith, the late Radical Premier of Queensland, pointed out in an admirable address delivered in Wales during his recent visit to this country—If the so-called Imperial Parliament is to retain any of its imperial character, and to hold its rightful position as the paramount British Legislative Assembly in the world, it is above all things necessary that it should remain the Parliament of the United Kingdom. Once disintegrate the "Home" Parliament, and we leave no central legislative body whose decisions would carry any weight outside the limits of its local territory; and though I am not an advocate for creating a brand-new centralised Imperial Parliament to which all the Colonies shall send delegates—preferring an alliance of Great Britain and her Colonies, by means of the "restoration" of some of the ancient prerogatives of the Crown—yet I think no calamity could be greater than to degrade the great historic Parliament of Westminster into the position of a mere local assembly. Sir Samuel Griffith was, in my opinion, absolutely correct in his prognostication of the evil of dividing the "Home" legislature and executive; and the English student of current Australian affairs may already notice in Sir Thomas M'Ilwraith's change of policy the direct result of Mr. Gladstone's deplorable surrender.

Under these circumstances, it seemed to me important that something approaching to an impartial estimate should be made of the Irish element in these British colonies. As a Victorian Englishman, I found it quite impossible to accept, on this question, the verdict of the two Victorian Irishmen; but I do not ask my readers to accept my views without thorough ratification, and I would even urge them to peruse the writings of my opponents before surrendering their judgments. I am quite aware of the distorting bias of all controversy, and in attempting—too eagerly it may be —to point out the mistakes of others, I have probably fallen into error myself.

I have only to add that Chapter VIII. was thought out and written many months before the imbroglio between the Colonial Office and the Local Government of Queensland. Rightly considered, as I have attempted to prove in the concluding Chapter, this event is a strong though unfortunate illustration of the necessity of the reform I have advocated.

In the Appendix (Note G) will be found a brief obituary of the late Dr. Hearn, of Melbourne, which originally appeared in the *Athenæum*, April 28, 1888. By a strange coincidence, as I was writing the reference to him, to be found on p. 142, the morning's paper was brought to me containing the cablegram from Melbourne, which announced the Australian philosopher's death. It was, of course, in the fewest possible words, nor had the Editor, as often happens, even in "colonial cases," supplemented Baron Reuter's intelligence by even the briefest biographical details. So I put my work aside and wrote down the bare facts of Dr. Hearn's distinguished career for the *Athenæum*.

It is a remarkable circumstance that, so far as I observed, this very imperfect sketch of Dr. Hearn was the only one that appeared in the London press. A "Society" paper, it is true, made the following suggestive comment on this still more suggestive silence on the part of the great daily journals: —"The news received within the last few days of the death of Dr. Hearn, in Melbourne, has by no means created the amount of attention in England which such an event should arouse. It does not tend to the much talked-of Imperial Federation when we see that the death of incomparably the greatest thinker and most profoundly learned man who has ever made his home in a British colony, calls forth so little comment in the centre of the Empire."

Had the death announced been that of some "tenth transmitter of a foolish face," on his Antipodean tour of vacant-mindedness, or that of an itinerant member of the House of Commons, of whom the most skilful flatterer would find it difficult to record any distinguishing moral or intellectual achievement, there would have been "biographies" in plenty. Nay—had Professor Hearn, instead of being a "mere colonial" who had written so admirable a work as *The Aryan Household*, been an Oxford or Cambridge Professor, his deeds would have been fully set forth at his death. Furthermore—and this is the rub—had Victoria been an independent State and not a mere "dependency," and had she thus nurtured a writer of the eminence of Dr. Hearn, and rewarded his great learning and his gigantic labours in codifying the laws of his country, by a seat in the local House of Peers, would not the British press have published some special account of such a public career? I lay stress on this, in itself, small matter, because the real moral of my book is, that if this complex and widely divided Empire is to be kept together, or rather, if it is to be consolidated into a real and not to remain a sham Empire, then it is essential that the dwellers at its periphery shall be under no "disabilities" as compared with their fellow-subjects at its centre. If we can bring about such a state of things, I venture to think that our race has sufficient common-sense to evolve some permanent plan whereby a world-wide alliance may be formed, based on those deep sentiments and ties which are thus eloquently dwelt upon by Bishop Thirlwall in his account of the colonisation of the ancient Greeks:—

"There was in most cases nothing to suggest the

feeling of dependence on the one side, or a claim of authority on the other. The sons, when they left their home to shift for themselves on a foreign shore, carried with them only the blessing of their fathers, and felt themselves completely emancipated from their control. Often the colony became more powerful than the parent, and the distance between them was generally so great as to preclude all attempts to enforce submission. . . . The place of such relations was supplied by the gentler and nobler ties of filial affection and religious reverence, and by usages which, springing out of these feelings, stood in their room, and tended to suggest them where they were wanting. . . . *But the most valuable fruit of this feeling was a disposition to mutual good offices in seasons of danger and distress.*"—(*History of Greece*, vol. ii. p. 98.)

Mainly through the progress of modern science, we British colonists are, according to Lord Salisbury, now also "*connected by the bands of mutual interest,*" which Bishop Thirlwall in those very words excluded from the ties which bound the Greek colonies to the parent State.

But I agree with Dr. Lang that much may be learned from a careful study of ancient Greek colonisation, in many respects a far nobler chapter in human history than our own: nor, while smiling at his arrogance, can I refrain from quoting the Doctor's really suggestive reminder to the supercilious modern Briton that, "Homer, the first of the Grecian poets, was an Ionian Greek colonist of Asia Minor; and so also was Herodotus, the first of her historians."

DOVER, *Christmas Day* 1888.

CONTENTS

I.

ROBERT LOWE IN SYDNEY,	p. 1-29
Arrival in Sydney, 1842,	3
Representative principle introduced in Sydney Council, 1842,	3
Sir George Gipps' new Council,	3
Dr. Lang on the first Australian Parliament,	4
Robert Lowe nominated M.L.C. by the Governor,	5
Wentworth and Lang,	5
Motion for separating Port Phillip from New South Wales,	5
Lowe's speech in favour of the motion,	6-8
Resignation,	8
The Atlas: a weekly Journal, 1843-45,	9
Its Contributors,	9
Opposition to the Governor and "Downing Street,"	9-13
Lord Sherbrooke's retrospect,	10
Softened feelings towards Sir Geo. Gipps,	10
Lowe's "rounded creed,"	11
Poems of a Life,	11
Lowe on the relations of Britain and her Colonies,	13, 14
The utterly unknown and doubly irresponsible Clerk,	13
Lowe's Remedies—Local Self-Government and Representation in the British Parliament,	13
Unwieldiness of a Common Parliament at Westminster,	14
"Council of the Empire,"	15
Bismarck on the Council of the Confederation of the German States,	15, 16
Colonial orators and Imperial councils,	16, 17
Robert Lowe on the Tractarian movement, Newman, Pusey, and Keble,	17, 18
The dominant Australasian Bishops,	18
Lowe's admiration of Dr. Arnold of Rugby,	17, 18
Sir James Martin's Creed,	18, 19
Lowe's theology and the *Sydney Morning Herald*,	20-23
Lowe on National Unsectarian Education,	23-26
Sir Richard Bourke—a retrospect—ablest of Australian Governors,	24, 25
Sir Richard as a Re-former,	24
Dr. Ullathorne supports Sir Richard Bourke's Education Scheme,	24, 25
Arouses Dr. Lang's bigotry,	25
Lang wrecks Sir Richard's measure,	25
Lowe converts Dr. Lang,	25
Lang's repentance—estimate of him as a public man,	26
Lowe's Colonial patriotism—a foremost Australian leader,	28
Elected member for Sydney in the Legislative Council, 1850,	28
Eight well-spent years under the "Southern Cross,"	28
Returns to England in 1851,	29

II.

SIR HENRY PARKES IN ENGLAND,	31-62
London Flesh Australian Grass,	31
A different type of Colonists now come "Home,"	32
The Colonial Exhibition and Conference, 1887,	32
Two Emigration Commissioners, 1860-61,	32, 33
Sir Henry Parkes and the Right Hon. W. B. Dalley,	33
Mr. Froude's *Oceana*,	34
His estimate of Australian public men,	34, 35
Description of Sir Henry Parkes,	35
Parkes Letters to *Sydney Morning Herald* in 1861,	33
Palmerston,	37
Disraeli, Brougham,	37
The American Civil War,	38-49
Apathy of the Birmingham audience towards manhood suffrage and ballot,	39
"Conservative reaction,"	39
Causes of the failure of Messrs. Parkes' and Dalley's emigration mission,	39-41
"Perhaps we could spare old Briggs,"	42
Parkes' sympathy with the North,	43
John Bright the true representative of the English Democracy—on America and on Ireland,	43
Beresford Hope and Tennyson both against the North,	43
Carlyle and Gladstone in favour of the South,	43
Personal influence of the Queen,	45
Death of the Prince Consort,	46
The *Trent* incident,	46-48
Christmas Eve, 1861,	46-49
Defenceless state of Australian colonies at that date,	49
A timely warning,	49
Disraeli on Prince Albert,	50, 51
Palmerston and "your Mr. Cowper,"	51
Colonial Defences Debate—Mr. Arthur Mills and "Sam Slick,"	51, 52
"Including Mr. Childers." Twenty-seven members present,	52
Social condition of England in 1862,	53
Panegyric on Cobden,	53
Odd speculations as to the future Statesmen,	54
A government consisting of "Cobden, Gladstone, and Stanley,"	54
Brougham's Adress at the Social Science Congress,	54-56
Brougham at the International Law Section with Travers Twiss and M. Garnier Pagès,	56
At the Social Science Soirée with Lord Shaftesbury,	56
"The aged poet Dean Milman,"	57
Palmerston a D.C.L., Oxford,	57
Sir Henry Taylor,	57-59
Wheatstone and Palmerston,	57-59
"A boy of fourscore,"	59
Rural Sights and Sounds,	59, 60
Value of a Colonial Observer,	61
Britain, America, and Australia,	61, 62

III.

LORD BEACONSFIELD AND YOUNG AUSTRALIA,	63-75
Effect of the cable,	63
Victorian Government and the broken cable,	64

News only received monthly (until Aug. 22, 1872) during the Franco-German War, 1870 —contrasted with the daily intelligence of the progress of the Russo-Turkish Campaign. 1877-78, . . . 64, 65
Russia and Australia, . . 65
Beaconsfield's Imperialism, . 66
"Patriotic Sonneteering," 66-68
Beaconsfield Demonstration in Melbourne, . . . 68-71
Speech by Mr. Service, . 69, 70
Mr. David Gaunson, . . 70
Comments of *Melbourne Argus*, 71-73
Meeting at Sydney, . . 71
Congratulations from Ballarat, Adelaide, and Newcastle, . 71
Causes of Disraeli's popularity, 74 and Mr. Gladstone's unpopularity in Australia, . . 75

IV.

AUSTRALIAN DEMOCRACY, 77-111
Australasia, seven self-governing democratic states claiming to be members of the Empire, ... 77
Qualifications necessary in a historian, . . . 78
Causes of the failure of more than one Colonial Historian, 77, 78
The anti-democratic bias, . 79
Wentworth's failure to create Colonial aristocracy, . . 79
His love of Australia and his imperial instincts, . . 79
Colonial autonomy and Colonial aristocracy, . . . 80
Wentworth's proposed Australian House of Lords, . . 80
Opposed by Robert Lowe in the British House of Commons, . 80

and by Henry Parkes in Sydney, ... 80
If it failed in New South Wales what chance had it in Victoria ? 81
Responsible Government in Victoria. 81
William Nicholson, . . 81
Vote by ballot, . . . 82
Democratisation of the constitution, ... 82
Mr. Rusden's *History of Australia*, ... 82
Secret of the rapid triumph of democratic principles, . . 83
The *anti-colonial* party, . . 83
Wentworth and Stawell exceptional, ... 84
Pessimism of the "upper-class" party. 85
Optimism of the democratic leaders, ... 85
An appeal to the Privy Council in 1869, ... 86
Bribers and bribed, . . . 86
Hon. George Higinbotham's reply, ... 86, 87
His faith in the body politic, . 87
Hostility of the English press, . 88
Mr. Finch-Hatton's *Advance Australia*, ... 88
His estimate of Australian public men, ... 89
"The *wealthy* lower orders," . 90
Mr. C. H. Pearson, Minister of Education, ... 91
Sir Charles Dilke's *Greater Britain*, . . . 91, 92
his chapters on Democracy and Protection, . . . 91
his estimate of Australian public men, ... 92
Aim of the democratic party, . 93

The Crown lands and squatters,	93
National education,	94
The Rev. J. Dalton on the Educational expenditure in Great Britain and the Colonies,	94
"Quill-driving" *versus* a handicraft,	95
General Gordon's wise forecast,	95
"Protection" in Victoria, Mr. Richard Heales and Sir Graham Berry,	96
"The logic of events,"	96
Effect of "free soup-kitchen," in Collingwood,	96
"What shall we do with our boys?"	97
Change in the Fiscal Policy of Victoria,	98
A Free-trade Cabinet introduces Protectionist tariff,	98
Inter-Colonial restrictive duties,	98
Can we have Imperial Free Trade with Protection against the world?	100
A British Zollverein,	100
Conversation between an Australian Protectionist and a great English Free-Trader,	100
"Titles for Colonists,"	101
Mr. Higinbotham's view,	102
"Impossible to discriminate their relative baseness,"	102
Messrs. Higinbotham and Francis decline a title,	102
The rest have accepted K.C.M.G. when offered,	102
Sir Robert Stout's remarkable Article,	103
Sir George Grey's views,	104
Opposed to Lord Carnarvon and Sir Michael Hicks-Beach,	105, 106
A merely "local" title illegal,	105
Should the Colonial or British Cabinet "advise" the Queen as to the distribution of honours in a self-governing Colony?	105
Sir R. Stout sums up controversy,	106
Obstruction in Colonial Parliaments,	108
Mr. Alfred Deakin's proposed remedy,	108
Mr. Service's opinion of Sir Chas. Warren and the Police in Trafalgar Square Riots, and murder of Sergeant Brett,	109
Why Colonial public-men can be outspoken,	110
Mr. Service on Armaments,	110
On the Conscription,	111
Australian Democratic Press, *Age* and *Leader*,	112
Australia and America,	112
Australian democracy must be met as a fact,	114

V.

AUSTRALIA AND IRISH HOME RULE,	115-134
A "solid" Australia,	115
Mr. Parnell and Mr. Rhodes,	115, 116
Mr. Parnell an "Imperial Federationist,"	116-119
Australian Irishmen may be Home-rulers,	119
No section analogous to the Irish American Dynamite Party,	119
Sir John O'Shanassy on the brothers Redmond,	119, 12
Effect of Mr. Gladstone's "conversion" on the Australian public mind,	120
Mr. Topp's Essay on English Institutions and the Irish Race,	121

CONTENTS

English Roman Catholics, . 123
Cardinal Manning, . . . 123
Celt and Teuton, . . . 124
Mr. Davitt on race, . . . 124
His "Mission of the Celts," . 125
Bismarck on race, . . . 126
Melbourne Review, . . . 126
The Highlander and Lowlander
  in Scotland, ... 129
Bismarck on the German and
  French character; the former
  applicable to the English and
  Lowland Scotch, . . . 130
The relations of England and
  Ireland in a sentence, . . 131
What is the Irish Problem? . 132

VI.

THE IRISH IN AUSTRALIA, 135-156
Irish population in Australia, . 135
"An Australian Example," . 135
"The Irish in Australia," . 136
Contrasted with "Victorian
  Year-Book." 136
Has the British majority played
  a minor *rôle*? 136
Victorian autonomy and Mr.
  Balfour, ... 137
Political capacity of the Irish
  in Australia, . . . 138
The Anglo-Irish and the Irish
  Celts, ... 138
Marcus Clarke's nationality, . 139
Wentworth, "the Australian
  Patriot," . . . 140, 141
Sir Wm. Foster Stawell, . . 141
Judge Molesworth, . . . 142
Wm. Edward Hearn, . . 142
George Higinbotham, . . 142
Their share in building up
  Victoria, ... 143
Early English Emigrants, . 144

Sir C. Gavan Duffy on the two
  Irish Sections, . . . 145
The purely Celtic Claims, 145, 146
"Why don't you stand?" . 146
I *am* an Englishman! . . 146
Disadvantages of belonging to
  the "Imperial and consoli-
  dating race,". . . . 146
The Celt a powerful factor in
  colonial affairs, . . . 147
"The Roman Catholic vote," 147
The English clergyman as a
  "wire-puller," . . . 148
"A political pessimist," . . 149
"Poll early, and Poll often," . 149
Acts of filial piety, . . . 150
Irish domestic servants, . . 150
An Englishman's anti-patriotic
  bias, ... 150
What do the Irish contribute
  to Australian or Imperial
  objects? 151
Australia's contribution to Irish
  famine fund, ... 151
Criminal Statistics, . . . 152
Autonomy of Victoria not ap-
  plicable to Ireland, . . 152
Major-General Sir Andrew
  Clarke, ... 152
Letter to John Bright, . . 154
Toleration the mark of the Vic-
  torian Era, ... 155
"The Weary Titan," . . 156

VII.

THE STATE SCHOOLMASTER, 157-187
Education in the colonies, . 157
"Free, secular, and compulsory," 157
Not necessarily purely secular, 157
Why was religion banished from
  Victorian schools? . . 158
Voluntary and Board schools in
  England, ... 159

Dr. Rigg and the "voluntary" Church of England schools, .	159
Australian difficulties and sociological differences, . .	160
Wilberforce Stephen's Education Act, and before, . .	160
Roman Catholic "Denominational" schools, . . .	160
The Policy of Bishop Perry and Bishop Moorhouse, . .	161
What is to be done with an alien race?	161
Assimilation by a "Common" Education, ...	161
Mr. Topp's views, . .	161
The Roman Catholic clergy much more hostile than the laity, .	163
Mr. Charles Fairfield's arguments, ...	163-166
Working of the Roman Catholic system in Spain and England, ...	164, 165
Criminal statistics, and the national and religious divisions of the people, .	165-167
Sir Robert Stout's views, .	166-168
"Waifs and Strays," . .	166
Crimes prevail not because of, but in spite of, religious belief,	168
Why religions not taught in State schools, . .	168-170
Anglican laity despite their bishops have built up the Australian National system,	169
"Common" schools, .	169, 170
Policy of the Roman Catholic Church in denouncing "mixed marriages,"	170
Real cause of the necessity for a "Common" system of State Education, . . .	171
Otherwise two permanently hostile races, . . .	171
Australia, — comparison with Scotland, ...	171
An "up-country" State schoolmaster, ...	172-177
Charles Wesley Caddy the bush philosopher, . . .	172-177
The late Mr. Geddie Pearse, "A Roger-Ascham of the Bush." His system of moral discipline, ...	176
Does the system justify the cost?	178, 179
Mr. Alex. Sutherland on the "Royal Readers," . .	179
Opinion of the working-class electors, and of many of the Protestant clergy, . . .	180
Attitude of the Church of England, ...	180, 181
A hope that the policy of Bishops Broughton and Moorhouse may be reversed,	181, 182
What has the Church gained? —only run the risk of "dis-Australianising" herself, .	182
Result if she would assist in the work of the "common" education of people, . .	183
She might restore some measure of religious instruction, and make herself the Church of Australia, ...	183
Are the State schools to be uprooted?—Opinion of an experienced Parliamentarian, .	184
The University Professor, .	185
Melbourne University, . .	186
Melbourne and Sydney not truly "so democratic as Oxford and Cambridge, . . .	187

VIII.

NATIVE AUSTRALIANS AND IMPERIAL FEDERATION, . 189-231

CONTENTS

Lord Carnarvon on Australian development, . . . 189
"*Australia for the Australians*," 189
Census Returns—Three out of every five persons in Victoria natives, ... 190
"Natives Association," . . 190
Racial and national speculations, 191
A new "Utopia," . . 191-194
Comments by an old Pioneer, 195-198
Dr. Hearn's "Aryan Household," 195, 196
Are the opinions of Young Australia day-dreams? . 199, 200
Echoes of the outworn traditions of Downing Street, . 201, 202
Sir Henry Taylor's minute to Lord Carlingford, 1865, 202, 203
Sir Henry's comments thereon, 1885, ... 204
Policy of Colonial independence originated with Sir James Stephen, but never countenanced in Australia, . 204, 205
Dr. Lang's " Coming Event," 204, 205
The typical colonist apathetic about Imperial Federation, . 206
Lord Salisbury's opening speech at Colonial Conference, 207-210
"A matter purely of self-interest," 210
Are the colonies safer in the Empire? 210
America after the Declaration of Independence, . . 210
Colonies in the 18th and 19th centuries, ... 212
Effects of steam and telegraph, 212
Bars to legislative union, . . 214
What is meant by Imperial Federation? 214
Sir Henry Parkes' scheme of local federation, . . 214, 217

Queensland and Western Australia omitted, . . 216-218
Mr. James Service's successful efforts to initiate a "bund" between Victoria, Queensland, Tasmania, and West Australia, ... 217
"Foreign Pressure," . . 218
New South Wales, South Australia and New-Zealand stood out, ... 218
"The Phantom at Hobart," . 218
Imperial Federation a misnomer without Imperial Free-trade, 219
Victorian customs duties, . 219
Must we drift? . . . 220
The change of sentiment now shaping new Nationalities and combinations of peoples, . 220
George Borrow and the Spanish Alcalde, . . . 221
"The Grand Baintham," . . 221
South American Republics, 221, 222
Effect of the American Civil War, ... 222
The Republic of George Washington and that of M. Grévy, 223
The *crux* of the problem, . 223
Can the colonies be received on equal terms into an Imperial alliance? 223
The question of Colonial Governorships—The Queen to appoint direct on advice from the Self-governing Colonies, instead of the Governor being a Downing Street nominee, 224-231
Over-centralisation, . . . 230
Itinerant Councils, and peripatetic Secretaries-of-State, . 231

CONTENTS

IX.

THE MORAL OF QUEENSLAND
  IMBROGLIO, . . 233-252
The Queensland Governorship, 233
Sir Henry Blake, . . . 233
Sir Thomas M'Ilwraith, . . 234
Poaches on Sir Samuel Griffith's
  "Radical preserves," . . 234
Dispute with Sir Anthony Musgrave and with Lord Knutsford, ... 235
Utility of "scientific imagination," 236
Early and present-day politicians contrasted, . . 236-239
"Plato and the preaching friars,". 237
"*Colonial Jealousies and the Government*," . . . 239
Loyalists and Disloyalists, 240, 241
The Celtic element in Colonial Cabinets, . . . 241, 242
Mrs. Campbell Praed's *Policy and Passion*, . . . 247
"Thomas Longleat," Premier of "Leichardt's-Land," . 247
Sir Thomas M'Ilwraith's "Opportunism," . . . 245
Mr. Gladstone's "Idolatry of the Immediate," . . . 246
Sir Thomas M'Ilwraith and Sir William Harcourt, . 245, 246
Programme of the National Party in Queensland, . 248, 249
Mr. Gowen Evans on the Irish Home-Rule Party in the colonies, . . . 249-250
The "little finger,". . . 250
The Victorian vote on Colonial Governorships—Moral, 251

APPENDICES.

A. ROBERT LOWE ON THE DISABILITIES OF COLONISTS, . 253
B. SIR C. GAVAN DUFFY'S "ROYAL COMMISSION," . 258
C. THE COLONIAL OFFICE AND THE "FOREIGN NOBLEMEN," 263
D. RELIGION AND IRISH HOME RULE, ... 267
E. EDUCATION IN AUSTRALIA, . 271
F. "A TYPICAL AUSTRALIAN STATESMAN," . . . 276
G. THE LATE W. E. HEARN, . 280
H. THE LATE WILLIAM BEDE DALLEY, ... 283

AUSTRALIA AND THE EMPIRE.

CHAPTER I.

ROBERT LOWE, VISCOUNT SHERBROOKE, IN SYDNEY.

In attempting to give, in the compass of a short book, some general account of the interdependent relations between "Australia and the Empire," I think I may lessen my reader's labour, as well as my own, by opening with two retrospective sketches. In the first, which takes us back some forty years, I propose to give a brief, but hitherto unwritten narrative of the public life in New South Wales of one of the most brilliant of contemporary Englishmen. And this may be not unfitly followed by a description of the England of a quarter of a century ago, as seen by the distinguished Australian statesman who may be said to have commenced his public career in Sydney under the ægis of Lord Sherbrooke, and who is at the present time once again Prime Minister of New South Wales.

So quickly do events succeed one another in the nineteenth century, so multitudinous are our printed records, and so inexorable is the law by which bygone mental impressions are obscured by fresh ones, that the memorable Australian career of Robert Lowe seems already to have been relegated to the shadowy realm of ill-remembered tradition. One has only to ask one's best-educated friends, whether Englishmen or Australians, a few questions concerning " Robert Lowe in Sydney," to discover that this is no exaggeration. The present writer, in his search for evidence on a disputed point in early—or rather " mediæval "—Australian history, was somewhat astonished to learn that one of the most intelligent officials of the British Museum was quite unaware of the fact that Lord Sherbrooke had ever resided, much less been a public man, in the Colonies. It would, of course, be hardly possible to find an Australian, in any corresponding social position, so entirely ignorant of Lord Sherbrooke's career in New South Wales. But if catechised it would probably be found that his knowledge is exceedingly dim and shadowy, and could be summed up by saying that once upon a time Robert Lowe, now Viscount Sherbrooke, was a member of the old Sydney Legislative Council.[1]

Robert Lowe, "Barrister-at-Law, and Fellow of Magdalen," arrived in Sydney in 1842, during the governorship of Sir George Gipps. The early Colonial Governors were "advised" by a Council, and the representative principle had just been partially introduced into the constitution of this body in New South Wales. This was effected in 1842 under the *régime* of the late Lord Derby, then Lord Stanley, who, as Secretary of State, succeeded in passing the "Constitutional Act for the better government of New South Wales." The Council consisted of thirty-six members; six officials, six Crown nominees, and twenty-four elected on a property qualification, six of whom were for the province of Port Phillip, now the independent colony of Victoria. This, the inauguration of the parliamentary system, was an exciting time both for the Governor and for the colonists. The Rev. Dr. Lang, one of the six members for Port Phillip, who has been truthfully described as "the greatest Scottish-Australian public

---

[1] In what purported to be a summary of the history of the "First Centenary of Australia" (*National Review*), Mr. Henniker Heaton, M.P., expatiated on Tawell the "Quaker Murderer," and on the "Rum Hospital," but did not even mention the name of Robert Lowe!

man," gives a sketch of this early Sydney Parliament which is worth preserving :—

"As a General Election and a partially representative Legislature were new things under the sun in Australia, and as the crisis at which the first election took place was a peculiarly trying one for the colony, the interest excited in all quarters was intense, and the result was by no means unsatisfactory. Indeed, for general ability, for extent and variety of information available for the business of legislation, for manly eloquence, for genuine patriotism, and for energetic and dignified action, I question whether the first Legislative Council in New South Wales has ever been surpassed by any Legislature out of England in the British Empire."

To justify this high eulogium Dr. Lang proceeds to enumerate half a dozen leading names, including that of Robert Lowe, whom he characterises as "a barrister of super-eminent ability and of brilliant oratorical powers." How came the newly arrived Fellow of Magdalen, it may be asked, so quickly to find his way into the Sydney Parliament? When Sir George Gipps, the first Governor of New South Wales, who was "hampered," as he would have said, by a body of Representatives, contemplated the results of the first elections in Australia, he might well have been appalled. The political capacity and debating power in two members alone of the "Opposition," William Charles Wentworth and John Dunmore Lang, far exceeded all that could be brought against them by the entire Ministerial benches, officials and nominees combined. Sir George Gipps, though utterly self-willed, and therefore often impracticable, was a clever man, and by no means undiscerning as a judge of the capacity of others. In the young English barrister, who had so recently stepped upon the shores of Port Jackson, the much-harassed Viceroy thought he could detect an intellectual gladiator capable of holding his own even against Wentworth and Lang. Accordingly, on November 10th, 1843, his Excellency nominated "Robert Lowe, Esq., Barrister-at-Law," to a seat in the Legislative Council. But the new member, as the sequel will show, was not of the material out of which the pliant placeman is manufactured. On August 20th, 1844, a memorable debate took place in the Sydney Legislative Council. On that evening Dr. Lang brought forward his celebrated motion for "the separation of Port Phillip from New South Wales, and its erection into a distinct and independent colony." With the exception of the five other members for Port Phillip, he had only one supporter—and that was Sir George Gipps' new nominee. With characteristic egotism Dr. Lang merely records the fact, and pays but scant tribute to the independence of mind that could have prompted such a vote, or could have supported it by so memorable a speech as Robert Lowe delivered that evening. I will endeavour to supply the Doctor's deficiency, by quoting the opening sentences of an address that was alone sufficient to raise the level of the debate from a mere provincial wrangle into the rare region of statesmanlike deliberation and discussion.

"As a general rule," began the new nominee member, "the interests of the Colonies are not consulted by frittering them away into minute particles, but by combining as large a territory into a single State as could be effectually controlled by a single Government. I cordially agree in the abstract truth of the motto prefixed to the article in the newspaper of this morning that 'Union is Strength'; and I would extend that principle to the whole Colonial Empire of Great Britain. *I hold and believe that the time is not remote when*

Great Britain will give up the idea of treating the dependencies of the Crown as children to be cast adrift by their parent as soon as they arrive at manhood, and substitute for it the far wiser and nobler policy of knitting herself and her Colonies into one mighty Confederacy, girdling the earth in its whole circumference, and confident against the world in arts and arms." This truly Imperial outburst was uttered, be it observed, wellnigh half a century before the Imperial Federation League was dreamt of. Although, as a colonist, I cannot see my way to adopt any of the schemes that have lately been propounded for the more complete fusion of Great Britain and her Colonies, I think this eloquent sentence which Robert Lowe uttered so many years ago, in the old Legislative Council of Sydney, forms a fit and noble motto for all of us, whether Englishmen or colonists, who are loyal to our beloved Sovereign, and faithful to the obligations and traditions of our common race and heritage. As such I have adopted it as the motto of this book.

After giving utterance to this lofty Imperial aspiration, the gifted orator, taking up the special point of Dr. Lang's motion, went on to say:—

"Neither can I agree that the separation [of Port Phillip] would be otherwise than injurious, in some extent, at least, to New South Wales. It implies the loss of a fertile and wealthy province already paying much more into the Treasury than it drew out of it; and I am also fearful that a separation might be attended with that animosity and ill-feeling which are so apt to prevail between neighbouring States, and that the result might be a war of tariffs and restrictive duties, which I hold in utter horror and aversion; but, still compelled by the force of Truth and Justice, I am bound to say that these considerations come too late."

On August 28th, exactly eight days after the delivery of this speech, Robert Lowe sent in his resignation as a nominee member of the Legislative Council of New South Wales. But he was already a man of mark, destined yet to play a leading part both as a journalist and a politician in the Colony, and soon to be acknowledged on the public platform as one of the most influential and powerful speakers on all the great questions then agitating the Australian public mind. Released from his anomalous position in the Council, Robert Lowe, like many an ambitious politician similarly placed, determined to influence his fellows and "educate his party" by means of the newspaper press. On November 30th, 1844, appeared in Sydney the first number of the *Atlas*, a weekly journal whose principles he formulated and whose policy he practically controlled. The literary ability of the new journal was undoubtedly high, for among the regular contributors there were, in addition to Lowe himself, a number of aspiring young men who subsequently attained to the highest positions in Australia—such as the Hon. William Forster, Sir Henry Parkes, Sir Archibald Michie, and the late Sir James Martin.[1] All of these, as well as their leader, were at that terribly aggressive "missionary age" of twenty-five to five-and-thirty, and were, of course, prepared not only to set Sir George Gipps and the local Executive to rights, but to readjust and rectify mundane affairs generally. The *Atlas* began its career as an open enemy, not only of the Governor of New South Wales, but also of the entire system of Colonial Government which emanated from Downing

---

[1] Perhaps a better proof could not be adduced of the literary ability of these contributors to the *Atlas* than the prominence justly accorded to several of them in Mr. Douglas Sladen's recently published anthology of "Australian Poets" (Griffith, Farran, and Co.)

Street. In kindly handing over to me some bound volumes of this remarkable Colonial newspaper, which teems with personal attacks upon the old Sydney Governor, whose memory is honoured by a bust and memorial tablet in Canterbury Cathedral,[1] Lord Sherbrooke, deprecating the bitterness of a long-past conflict, wrote :—

"It was always a great regret to me that I had been obliged to oppose Sir George Gipps so strongly, as he had been personally most kind."

To some rigid natures this softened confession of the veteran statesman may seem uncalled for, but it will appeal to those who, with increasing years, learn to doubt and mistrust themselves as well as others.

It may be seriously questioned whether any Government in the world was ever more persistently and artistically bespattered with printer's ink than was that of Sir George Gipps, for at least two years after the first publication of the *Atlas*. The great

[1] The inscription reads thus :—"In the adjoining cloisters are interred the remains of Lt.-Colonel Sir George Gipps, of the Royal Engineers, late Governor-in-Chief of New South Wales and its Dependencies, who died the 28th February 1847, aged 56 years, after an honourable and useful career of thirty-nine years in the Military and Civil Services of his country. He returned to England from the above colony impaired in health, and shortly afterwards expired in this city. Beloved, honoured, and regretted by all who knew him."

bulk of the weighty leading articles and pungent paragraphs were from Robert Lowe's own pen. He it was who alone, amongst this brilliant band of young journalists, had what has been called a "rounded creed." Rightly or wrongly, as befits the leader of a party, he had made up his mind (and was ready to make up the mind of everybody else) on all the problems that perplex, divide, and distract humanity. It is needless to say that the much-harassed Governor was unceremoniously dragged to the bar of public opinion and pilloried, with cruel regularity, every Saturday morning. Many of the matters upon which these ardent reformers differed from the Colonial Executive of the day were only of local concern, and have long since been settled and forgotten.

Strange to say, I find in a slender volume of verse, recently published in London, entitled *Poems of a Life*, by Lord Sherbrooke, several of the contributions that originally adorned the poets' corner of the *Atlas* in the years 1844-45; but often in a somewhat softened form. In one of the very earliest numbers poor Sir George Gipps was thus confronted by that dread "power" which, according to its chief invoker, was so speedily to overwhelm him:—

"It is now pretty well agreed," wrote the editor, "that public opinion is the power which does and ought to rule mankind. The most splendid fabrics of human policy—the Papacy of Hildebrand, the Aristocracies of Venice and England, and the Empire of France, have crumbled into dust before its silent power."

The "local application" of this asserted law of human development, so Sir George Gipps was curtly informed, was to "dissolve the Council and let the country select a new organ which will represent its opinions; and then obey it. If you dare not dissolve, and will not obey—Resign."

This drastic remedy was further enforced by a set of characteristic verses entitled "The Tyrant's Lesson," in which the same writer, under the pseudonym of Machiavelli, imparted to the poor Colonial magnate some very sinister advice :—

"Keep thy people in slavery; straiten their flocks,
  Be miser of desert and niggard of sand,
Extort the full price of the Government rocks,
  And the gum-tree that shelters the fountainless land.

Thus ignorant, drunken, impoverished and tame,
  With nought that is manly, enlightened, and free,
With nought of the land whence they sprang but the name,
  Perchance they may fawn on a ruler like thee."

After reading such gentle effusions as these, Sir George Gipps must have felt that the great "power of public opinion," so far as his late nominee member was its interpreter, was thoroughly antagonistic, not only to him personally, but to the entire system of government then in vogue in the Colony.

But it was in dealing with the wider question of the relations existing between England and her Colonies that Robert Lowe's pen found its fullest scope. It should be borne in mind that he wrote before the era of "responsible government" in the Colonies. The outlying possessions of England were then governed, or rather misgoverned, by despatches from Downing Street, which, as Lowe pointed out, were not the work of the Secretary of State, or even of the chief permanent officials, but emanated from "the doubly-irresponsible, because utterly unknown and obscure, Clerk."

The account he gives of the manner in which our whole Colonial Empire was governed forty years ago can only be applicable now to the straggling remnant of Crown Colonies.[1] For the evils under which New South Wales was then, according to the

[1] See Appendix C, "The Colonial Office and the Foreign Nobleman," p. 262.

Atlas, deeply groaning, the remedies suggested were (1) Local self-government, and (2) Representation in the British Parliament. The former has long since been achieved, and has worked, like other mundane contrivances, with more or less success. In defence of the latter measure, the chief panacea of our present-day Imperial Federationists, Robert Lowe addressed an argument which had much more weight before the Colonies achieved autonomy. "If," he wrote, "the Colonial Secretary were to be called to account, in the face of the House and the country, for the freaks and misconduct of his clerks, he would then quickly discover that however competent one person may be to administer the *patronage*, one person cannot manage the *affairs* of forty Colonies. A division of labour would ensue as soon as responsibility was really felt, the reign of clerks would terminate, and that of responsible ministers would begin."

To my mind, at least, it seems that what I may call the unwieldiness of a common Parliament at Westminster for so enormous and widely-divided an Empire, far more than outweighs such arguments in its favour. This is strongly emphasised just at present, when a large party in the State loudly declare that a single Parliament cannot perform the legislative work of these two small contiguous islands. I believe that on this point they are wrong; but the evil is in our one-sided development of the Parliamentary system. If ever we are to have a Council of the Empire it will certainly have to be conducted more on the principles of the old Councils of the German Confederation, for which even Prince Bismarck—that honest hater of Parliaments—had a good word. I would like Lord Sherbrooke's opinion on the great Chancellor's views, and will, at the risk of the digression, quote Bismarck's words for the benefit of the Imperial Federation League:—

"The gift of oratory," remarked the greatest statesman of modern times, " has ruined much in Parliamentary life. Time is wasted because every one who feels ability in that line must have his word, even if he has no new point to bring forward. Speaking is too much in the air and too little to the point. Everything is already settled in committees: a man speaks at length, therefore, only for the public to whom he wishes to show off as much as possible, and still more for the newspapers who are to praise him. Oratory will one day come to be looked upon as a generally harmful quality, and a man will be punished who allows himself to be guilty of a long speech. We have one body," he continued, "which admits no oratory, and has yet done more for the German cause than almost any other—the Council of the Confederation. I remember that at first some attempts were made in that direction. But I put a stop to them. I said to them something like this:—'Gentlemen, we have nothing to do here with eloquence and speeches intended to produce conviction, because every one brings his conviction with him in his pocket—I mean his instructions. It is so much time lost. I propose that we confine ourselves here to the statement of facts.' And so it was; no one again made a long speech. We get on so much the faster with our business; and the Council of the Confederation has really done a great deal."[1]

Be sure if our Colonial orators were thus to have their mouths stopped they would not want to come from the uttermost parts of the earth to Westminster; nor under any working scheme of Imperial unity should it be necessary, except occasionally for consultative purposes. On any general question of Imperial policy the representatives of Melbourne, Ottawa, or Sydney, should have their "instructions," which they could telegraph in the fewest possible

---

[1] *Bismarck in the Franco-German War*, by Dr. Busch, vol. ii. pp. 299-300.

words to the central authority, thereby saving both time and money as well as a wearisome journey, and a still more wearisome flow of words. But I admit that to keep the various parts of the Empire in touch with each other, it would be well to hold consultative councils of delegates from its various sections, something like the Church Congresses, and like them these Councils should meet each time in a different centre.

Some cynic has said that "the last infirmity of noble minds" is theology. Certainly, to judge from Robert Lowe's contributions to the *Atlas*, he, in the years 1844-45, gave no inconsiderable amount of thought to that remarkable religious revival in England, generally known under the name of "Puseyism." As an antidote to the sacerdotal doctrines of Newman, Pusey, and Keble, whom he appears to have equally detested, we find him expatiating, week after week, on the theological and philosophical excellencies of Dr. Arnold of Rugby.[1] Like many Liberal Churchmen of half-a-century ago he failed to realise that the amazing development of modern physical science would shatter any creed raised on a quasi-rationalistic basis, like that

[1] He even reprinted *in extenso* the once famous article from the *Edinburgh Review*, on "Oxford Malignants," by Dr. Arnold, to the amazement, one would think, of the remote Colonial reader.

of the so-called "Broad Church." It is therefore not to be wondered at that he failed to foresee that the Church of England would owe its enormously enhanced position in the present day more to the teaching and example of Pusey than to that of any other man of our age; whereas the influence of Dr. Arnold, who was not only an equally excellent man, but from his own standpoint as true a Christian and as firm a Churchman, has all but entirely passed away. It would be amusing, but perhaps not edifying, to quote some of the comments Lowe indulged in on the leading "sacerdotalists" whose baneful influence he could trace in the public conduct of the three dominant Bishops then in Australasia—Broughton,[1] Selwyn, and Nixon.

But I cannot refrain from pointing out that Robert Lowe, by these "liberal expositions," appears to have made a notable "convert" in the person of Sir James Martin, the late Chief-Justice of New South

---

[1] In the aisle of Canterbury Cathedral, near the great west door, and adjoining the memorial to Sir George Gipps, is the tomb with its recumbent figure of this the first and, with the exception of Bishop Selwyn, the greatest of Australasian prelates—*Primus Episcopus Sydneiensis, et Australiæ Metropolitanus.* So repose the remains of the two men who, in Robert Lowe's time, were the official head of Church and State in Australia

Wales, who was then on the literary staff of the *Atlas*. He it is of whom Mr. Froude gives such a flattering picture in *Oceana*, declaring that "if Sir James Martin had been Chief-Justice of England he would have passed as one of the most distinguished occupants of that high position." Sir James was by birth an Irishman, and baptized a Roman Catholic, but, from his intimate connection with the *Atlas*, he seems to have imbibed some of his early leader's freedom of theological speculation, for he lived all his later life outside the pale of that Church, steadily refusing to be reconciled with it even in his last hours. He was buried some two years ago in Sydney, by Dr. Barry, the present Primate of Australia, with the rites of the Anglican Church, though I am not aware that he was ever formally received into that communion.

It is also pleasant to be able to mention one instance in which Robert Lowe turned his "theological bias" to practical political account. In defending a once notorious criminal, Lowe, quite within his rights as an advocate, had pleaded that the murderer was either a lunatic or not a free agent; and the leading journal in the Colony, the *Sydney Morning Herald*, to speak metaphorically, held up its hands in pious horror. This was somewhat awkward, as Lowe was offering himself at the time as a candidate for the Legislative Council. He at once wrote to the *Herald*, and demanded to know in what particular his speech at the trial had impugned "the first principles of Christianity," and " what those principles of Christianity are to which you consider those doctrines to be opposed ?"

The astute reader will at once notice the dark and dreadful trap, but the editor, who was emboldened by some remarks which had fallen from the judge at the trial, accepted Lowe's challenge, and rambled on about Freewill and Necessity; rashly maintaining that if the former were denied to man, the Christian theory became a mere farce. The editor's statement is very pious and very commonplace, but Lowe's retort was novel and refreshing, and is perhaps unequalled in the brief annals of Australian polemics. It begins thus :—

"To the Editors of the *Sydney Morning Herald*.

" GENTLEMEN,—When I asked you to point out the doctrine of Christianity to which my speech was opposed, I expected to be referred to something held by Christians in common, and not to the doctrine of the Wesleyan sect, for it may be, gentlemen, that I am not a Wesleyan Methodist, and, not to keep you in further suspense, the fact is that I am a member of the Church of England. You are not ignorant of this, but you probably are ignorant of the Articles of that Church."

He thereupon "subjoined a copy" of the Tenth Article, and referred the unhappy editor to the Eleventh, Twelfth, and Seventeenth, which "show clearly that though *you* may consider the foundation of the whole system of Divine government to be man's free agency and consequent responsibility, the Church of England, whose Articles I have repeatedly subscribed, does not."

After repeating what he had said at the trial, as to the hereditary taint in the murderer's family, with a scientific lucidity that Dr. Maudsley might envy, he wound up his letter in the following slashing and effective style :—

"It was an aspiring wish of the Arian Milton to justify the ways of God to man, but it is a wish that can never be accomplished; the existence of evil will meet the presumptuous speculator at every turn and fling him back into the shallow nothingness of his nature. Dangerous it were, says the eloquent and judicious Hooker, for the feeble brain of man to wade far into the doings of the Most High, whom although to know be life, and joy to make mention of His name, yet our soundest knowledge is to know Him, not indeed as He is, neither can we know Him, and our safest eloquence concerning Him is our silence, when we confess without confession that His glory is inexplicable, His greatness above our capacity and reach. He is above and we upon earth, therefore it behoveth our words to be wary and few.

"And now, gentlemen, I have done with you. I ask you for principles, and you give me inferences. I ask you for Christianity, and you give me Methodism. You are now at full liberty to inter *this* slander by the side of his deceased brother of last week, and as you seem rather at a loss for something to urge against me at the present time, I will take the liberty of suggesting a few topics myself. I ride a very ugly horse: that clearly proves me to be an atheist, for who else could be so insensible to the beauties of the noblest animal of the creation? I live in a very small house, which clearly shows I must have a very contracted mind; and I am sometimes known to play at billiards, which shows a strong, though, it may perhaps be expedient in candour to admit, not quite fully developed propensity for gambling.—I am, Gentlemen, your obedient Servant,"

"ROBERT LOWE."

Robert Lowe was the foremost advocate, during all the time he was in Sydney, of a national unsectarian system of public education, as opposed to the old denominational system which formerly prevailed. I propose to deal separately with this great subject of public education in a subsequent section. But no sketch, however brief, of Robert Lowe's career in Sydney would be at all adequate which failed to recognise his unwearying services as an educational reformer. To understand the "Education Question" in the time of Sir George Gipps, it is necessary to glance for a moment at the condition of affairs under his predecessor, Sir Richard Bourke, incomparably the ablest of the early Governors of Australia. Sir Richard's career does not, I regret to state, come within the scope and compass of the present work, for he belongs to what may be called "ancient" or pre-Parliamentary Australian annals. But it would be well for all, English and Australians alike, to bear in mind what a number of admirable "*re-forms*"—in the true sense of the word, as being constructive rather than destructive in character—Sir Richard Bourke effected without the aid of either patriotic orators or public meetings. He practically established freedom of the press in New South Wales; and, as the inscription on his statue in the Domain, Sydney, declares with more historical accuracy than is usual, "He established religious equality on a just and firm basis, and sought to provide for all, without distinction of sect, a sound and adequate system of national education." And, be it remarked, he effected these reforms in the spirit of a far-seeing statesman, for his personal predilections were, as those who have read the *Life* of his friend Bishop Jebb, of Limerick, may remember, entirely with his own religious communion, which he thus deposed from its pride of place. In his earnest endeavour to introduce what is known as the Irish national system of education into New South Wales, Sir Richard Bourke failed. In the attempt he was warmly supported by Dr. Ullathorne, the justly respected Roman Catholic Vicar-

General, afterwards Bishop of Birmingham, who, it may be presumed, favoured the national unsectarian system as a direct attack on Anglican prerogatives in the colony. Whatever may have been the cause, Dr. Ullathorne's support of unsectarian education is worth bearing in mind when we come to the subject of the State schoolmaster.

It was, however, owing to Dr. Ullathorne's support, which roused the effective bigotry of Dr. Lang, that Sir Richard Bourke's statesmanlike measure was wrecked. Subsequently, under the vigorous tutelage of Robert Lowe, Dr. Lang learnt that he had done a very foolish thing in opposing Sir Richard Bourke, and had simply played into the hands of Dr. Ullathorne's co-religionists. Dr. Lang repented in sackcloth and ashes, and from that time became a rabid "Nationalist" on the education question, and "a devoted disciple" of Lowe. In his entertaining but oppressively egotistical *History of New South Wales* appears the following suggestive passage :—

"I have already observed that one of the great questions which engaged the attention of the first Legislative Council, during the year 1844, was the question of education ; on which there had been a

Select Committee appointed in the earlier part of the session, under the chairmanship of Robert Lowe, Esq., now member of Parliament for Kidderminster. That Committee had reported strongly in favour of the National system: and I endeavoured on the occasion, as a member of the Committee as well as of the Council, to atone as much as possible for the opposition I had given to the establishment of Sir Richard Bourke's system in the year 1835."

Despite all his good intentions Dr. Lang was unable to undo the evil of his former rash and bigoted opposition, and the result was that no national system of education worthy of the name was carried into law in New South Wales, until Sir Henry Parkes passed the Public Schools Act of 1867.

I would not like this unqualified censure of Dr. Lang to stand without adding that despite the grave error of judgment displayed in his early career to the wreckage of a carefully matured and statesmanlike system of public education, there is no public man in my opinion, with the solitary exception of Wentworth, who has played so important a part in the "making of Australia"; and I venture on this assertion while fully conscious that Dr. Lang's mental endowments and political capacity were of a distinctly commoner type than those of the subject of this brief memoir, or of his great Australian rival.

Public feeling at Sydney in 1846 was at fever-heat. Sir George Gipps had publicly notified, six years before this date, that criminal transportation to the Colony had ceased. But although an overwhelming number of the colonists had hailed this new departure in the policy of the Home Government with intense delight, there was a small but influential minority who were grimly dissatisfied. Mr. Gladstone, who was then for a short time Secretary of State for the Colonies, had forwarded a somewhat enigmatical despatch to Sir George Gipps with regard to the renewal of transportation. This led to a state of the wildest public excitement in the colony, and at the monster meetings which were held in Sydney no speaker was listened to with more delight, and certainly none was more deserving of attention, than Robert Lowe.[1] In fact, from the years 1844 to 1850 no colonial public man was more active or more influential than he. On all the great questions of the hour he was on the

[1] See Appendix A.

platform, as in the press, a vigilant upholder of the rights of the people, and a particularly keen critic of the Colonial Office. At a public meeting held on January 20th, 1848, at Sydney, Earl Grey's proposal to "amend" the Constitution of New South Wales, in view of the separation of Port Phillip, was criticised with great trenchancy by Mr. Lowe. He detected an anti-popular flavour in everything that emanated from the Liberal Colonial Secretary, and on this occasion, as indeed on all others, he entirely carried his hearers with him.

In 1850 Robert Lowe received the well-merited honour of being elected to represent Sydney in the Legislative Council of New South Wales, but the following year he resigned his seat, and returned to England, and began his great English Parliamentary career.

Viscount Sherbrooke, it is true, spent only some eight years of his life at the Antipodes, but those years were of the very prime of his manhood. By his commanding talents and political capacity, he, in that brief space of time, divided with Wentworth the honours of the Senate and the emoluments of the Bar. As a colonial public man he experienced that most exhilarating of all feelings, the consciousness that his heart throbbed with the great heart of the people. And yet, if one turns to his public utterances, one sees that he never descended to mere clap-trap, and rarely appealed to any but the nobler feelings of our common nature.

Few public men, English or colonial, can, if at all self-critical, look back upon any eight consecutive years of their life with more satisfaction than Lord Sherbrooke may regard those passed under the Southern Cross. Singled out almost on his landing by a particularly astute ruler for the coveted honour of a place at his council-table, the brilliant young English barrister, on the first opportunity, showed that he regarded the interests of the people amongst whom he had come to live as of paramount importance. It was not the way, as other distinguished exiles well knew, to place and pension; but it should give to Robert Lowe, a high name and an enduring recognition in the annals of Australia.

CHAPTER II.

SIR HENRY PARKES IN ENGLAND.

If, as I venture to think, an Imperial lesson may be learned from the Colonial public career of Lord Sherbrooke, so too may we perhaps learn something from the "impressions of England" formed during a prolonged visit by the present Prime Minister of New South Wales.

It is always good "to see ourselves as others see us"; but this is especially the case, it seems to me, with the members of so vast and so widely divided an Empire as ours.

There was never a time when a certain class of successful colonist did not come "Home"—as he fondly calls the mother-country—to fashionably flicker out his latter days. "A good deal of London flesh," once said Sir Archibald Michie, "is Australian grass." But a very different type of colonist, especially within the last few years, has been in the habit of coming to England, as a bird of passage merely, always regarding his particular Colony as his real "home." The recent Colonial Exhibition at South Kensington brought a good number of such visitors to England. Still more important from a political point of view was the subsequent assembling of the Colonial Conference under Sir Henry Holland, now Lord Knutsford. Then we had in London a number of prominent Colonial public men, each of whom regarded his individual colony as his true sphere of public labour, and none of whom desired to be merged in the ordinary ruck of the purely British population. From an Imperial point of view, the opinions that these men brought to Downing Street, and still more those that they carried back from that *arcanum*, must be regarded as of the very first importance. Still, after mature consideration, I have chosen rather to take my sketch of the "Australian in England" from a period sufficiently remote to give the effect of perspective.

Over a quarter of a century ago a pair of very remarkable Australian colonists visited England in the capacity of Emigration Commissioners. Had they been ordinary individuals they would doubtless have been styled Emigration agents, but they were prominent politicians; and prominent politicians, even in the most democratic communities, are wont to bestow upon themselves high-sounding titles, just as in England they raise one another to the Peerage. These two gentlemen were Mr.—now Sir—Henry Parkes, G.C.M.G., the present veteran Prime Minister of New South Wales, and the late Right Hon. William Bede Dalley—then plain Mr. Dalley, but who was to become the first Australian Member of the Privy Council—an unique distinction bestowed upon him for sending a Colonial contingent to the support of the British troops in the Soudan.

During the visit of Mr. Parkes and Mr. Dalley to England, from the autumn of 1861 to the summer of 1862, the former, it seems, contributed a slender series of monthly letters to the columns of the *Sydney Morning Herald*.[1] Quite apart from any mere literary merit, these letters have a distinct sociological value as a record of the fresh impressions made on the mind of a colonial politician of exceptional ability, on his return, after an absence of twenty years, to his native land. It is perhaps due to the English reader that a few preliminary remarks should be made concerning the

---

[1] A selection of these Letters was published by Messrs. Macmillan in London under the title *Australian Views of England*.

personality of their Australian visitor and critic. I believe that Sir Henry Parkes is one of that small band of public men at the Antipodes who would have made not merely an evanescent mark in the House of Commons, but who, in time of trial or at a national crisis, might have left a name in the history of his country. I would here remark that Mr. Froude's brilliantly written and otherwise deservedly popular *Oceana*, to my mind, conveys a very false impression as to the worth and relative importance of Colonial public men. Mr. Froude professes to write merely of the men with whom he actually came in contact, and as he was only some six weeks all told on the vast Island-Continent, he seems to have decided, not without wisdom, to glean his information from the Viceroys, and the one or two chief politicians in office. Mr. Dalley, who at this time was in the throes of sending the Soudan contingent, naturally appeared a much more important figure to Mr. Froude than Sir Henry Parkes, who was in the cold shade of unpopular opposition. Similarly in Victoria, Mr. Froude has much to say about the mere passing politicians of the hour, but did not, I believe, meet such a quite exceptional public man as the Hon.

George Higinbotham, the present Chief-Justice, who is about the last person in the world to offer himself as a subject even to the most celebrated of literary limners. To revert to Sir Henry Parkes, who, I must say, does not receive justice at the hands of Mr. Froude, I repeat that he is, and has been for many years, the most remarkable public figure in New South Wales.

Born over seventy years ago, of humble parents, under the shadow of Stoneleigh Abbey, Sir Henry Parkes received the rudiments of his education at the village school in the beautiful county of Shakespeare and George Eliot. Like almost all those adventurous spirits who have left their mark in the annals of Australia, he migrated thither in his early manhood. His long public career in New South Wales has been one of ceaseless strife and frequent vicissitude, and it is no secret that as in the case of greater statesmen he has shown himself more capable of controlling the affairs of the community than of managing his own. Quickly emerging from obscurity in the then rising city of Sydney, Parkes proved his strength when there were at least two giants in the land—Robert Lowe, then in the early vigour of his splendid intellect, with fame and fortune to achieve, and William Charles Wentworth, whose genius was quite as commanding, and perhaps more statesmanlike. After the return of Lowe to England and the retirement of Wentworth, it was inevitable that a man with the political instincts and combative attributes of Parkes should quickly come to the fore under the free constitution which Wentworth had devised for the colony.

Standing well over six feet in height, with his large leonine head, and huge shaggy locks now whitened by half a century of strenuous public life, Sir Henry Parkes presents a striking and commanding figure. Far from the fashion-plate type, either in face or form, this Australian, even when seen in the most aristocratic of London drawing-rooms, commands the glances of admiration; for his appearance is neither commonplace nor conventional, and in his manner there is no vestige of vulgarity. The man's mind too, distorted as it has often shown itself by the born politician's insatiable love of power and popularity, is in many respects large and even catholic in its aims and predilections. I have only to add that Sir Henry Parkes has been three times Prime Minister of

New South Wales, and that now, in his seventy-fourth year, he again grasps in his capable hands the helm of public affairs in that great dependency.

Let us turn now to the old files of the Sydney newspaper, and see what picture this even then distinguished Australian formed of the England of twenty-five years ago, when Lord Palmerston, in his eightieth year, was jauntily governing the country, with Mr. Gladstone as Chancellor of the Exchequer, and Mr. Disraeli as leader of the Opposition; when the Prince Consort's sudden death left the Queen a bereaved woman, and removed from the conduct of England's complex affairs a most clear, searching, and unbiassed intellect; when the grand vitality of Lord Brougham was fast flickering out like a spent flame, while Bright and Cobden were in the zenith of their political activity; when Carlyle and Tennyson were on the rising tide of literary pre-eminence—and when our kinsmen of America were rent asunder by the most Titanic Civil War in the annals of mankind.

The English reader will be good enough to bear in mind that the mission of Messrs. Parkes and

Dalley to England in 1861-62 was to induce emigrants to select Australia as their future home. Sir Henry's series of letters open with a suggestive reference to the re-awakened antagonism throughout England to democratic institutions, which he regards as a result of the American Civil War.

"The civil discord in America," he observes, "to an extent unjust to the Americans, has repelled and partly terrified the public mind; and anything that was felt to savour of American democracy, would, I verily believe, be ill-received in any great gathering of the people. The other day I heard a popular lecturer, Mr. George Dawson, discoursing to an audience of at least a thousand persons on the American troubles, and he indulged in some sharp ridicule of universal suffrage, which was received with loud cheers and merriment. The same indifference to what would have elicited a tempest of cheering from any meeting a few years ago, was manifested a night or two back at a great meeting assembled to hear an address from one of your Colonial Commissioners, Mr. Parkes."

"I suppose," he continues, with the charming *insouciance* of newspaper anonymity, "Mr. Parkes considered it part of his duty to describe the political institutions of the colony, and though his address was well received and frequently applauded, when he explained that the Legislative Assembly was elected by manhood suffrage and the ballot, not a single cheer was heard. Mr. Parkes was addressing at least 5000 people, chiefly Birmingham artisans, who, twenty-two years ago, waged civil war for the five points of the People's Charter."

Such an experience was well calculated to make the Australian orator, who has always been a Liberal of what Mr. Chamberlain would call "the older and the nobler type," pause and ruminate as to whether there was a widespread Conservative reaction in England. He noted with a politician's eye the currents and variations of public opinion. He observed, for instance, notwithstanding the matchless platform oratory of John Bright, that he received "no such ovation as Russell, Palmerston, Carlisle, Stanley, Lytton, Pakington, who seemed the ascendant stars." Cobden he heard bitterly reviled at a *table-d'hôte*, and no indignant voice raised in his defence.

"To my mind," remarks the sturdy Australian, " there is something of glaring injustice towards the men who have sprung from the people's own ranks, and of degrading fickleness of opinion in the people themselves in this apparent mistrust and neglect of their old friends." He tries to console himself with the somewhat bitter reflection that "it is not conservative reaction in the old party sense of the term, but the action of a shopocratic conservatism of modern growth, combined with a sprinkling of flunkeyism and a larger leaven of political infidelity." The writer explains that by this last phrase he means that the intelligent English artisans had come to see that "political agitation very inadequately supplies the daily wants of a family, and ministers but little to the enjoyment of life."

But over and above all these reasons for this strange condition of English public opinion, the Australian shrewdly detected the rooted dislike of Republican America, heightened into hysteria by the spectacle of the terrible internecine conflict. It is certainly a singular illustration of the law of reflex action that, owing to the American Civil War, the two Australian Emigration Commissioners should have been so completely baffled in England. The most influential English journals pointed to the struggle across the Atlantic as the inevitable outcome of a state of things where one man was, at least in theory, as good as another. What America to-day is, argued these wiseacres, Australia will become to-morrow.

Clearly, this pair of Commissioners from a far-off democratic colony had come to England—" Home," as they affectionately termed it—at a very untoward time. Famine stalked abroad in the land, yet the people turned a deaf ear to the eloquent pair who would fain have charmed them away to the antipodean land of plenty. But the Emigration Commissioners though baffled were not beaten, and the readers of the Sydney journal were assured, by its energetic correspondent, that Mr. Dalley, all undaunted, was "agitating the home counties"; while " Mr. Parkes was moving about in the manufacturing districts."

Perhaps History presents no other record of a mission, undertaken by men of such peculiar fitness for it, that ever failed so utterly. It has been asserted, probably with some slight exaggeration, that Messrs. Parkes and Dalley did not induce a single English family to emigrate to Australia. A friend of Mr. Dalley used to repeat a story which that admirable *raconteur* was fond of relating on his return to Sydney. He had been dining at a pleasant parsonage in Kent—for though of an alien faith, the brilliant Australian-Irishman was partial to the society of that all but extinct type of English cleric who knew his Aristophanes better than his Chrysostom, and who was in reality the clean and decorous Anglican analogue of that historic clerical worldling, the "French Abbé" of the last century. The evening wore merrily on without so much as an allusion to the great emigration question. Suddenly, prompted by a sense of duty, or perhaps by a vision of his colleague's greater success as a fisher of men in the crowded streets of Birmingham and Manchester, Mr. Dalley said:—

"Cannot you help me in selecting some really deserving fellows in your parish who would be likely to make good colonists?"

The jovial parson paused, to give the subject thought, toying lightly with his glass of port.

"I know no one," said he, after a while, "except old Briggs; he is getting on in years, and is very asthmatic, and too fond of malt liquor. *I think, perhaps, we could spare him.*"

After this Mr. Dalley gave over haunting parsonages as a means of finding hardy pioneers to people the waste places of his great colony.

Reverting to Sir Henry Parkes' letters, there seems to me a real historic interest in his conviction that his want of success was the result of the American Civil War. Sir Henry himself held very strong opinions concerning that awful fratricidal quarrel. He took his stand beside John Bright, who, on the question of the dismemberment of the United States, as on that of the separation of Great Britain and Ireland, may be regarded as the true representative of the English-speaking world. Hardly a letter that Sir Henry sent off to Sydney but was filled with expressions of profound sympathy for the North. As we know there was a very large number of high-minded and intelligent Englishmen whose sympathies were just as strong on the other side; the late Mr. A. Beresford Hope,[1] for instance. We know that after his own country and his Church, the warmest sympathies of that generous, high-minded English gentleman were given to the Southerners, who, in his eyes, were the Transatlantic Cavaliers fighting

---

[1] Tennyson and Carlyle might also be cited. "Spent the evening at the house of Mr. Woolner, sculptor, with Tennyson, a quiet, simple man, who smoked a pipe and drank hot punch with us. He deplores the American War, and talks of the Yankees, whom he detested."—Diary of J. R. Thompson, *Lippincott's Magazine*, November 1888.

for their rights against the aggressive, narrow-minded, shop-keeping Puritans of New England. Sir Henry Parkes, however, like the rest of us who are at all in earnest, could only see his own side of the question. But his letters throw a vivid sidelight on public opinion in England a quarter of a century ago, which, I think, is not without interest to Englishmen, Americans, and Australians of to-day.

"It is curious to note," he writes, "the ill-informed and ill-natured remarks on the Civil War in America which are made among the trading classes. If you meet with a manufacturer or a travelling factor in a hotel or railway carriage, he is sure to amuse you with some clumsy and ignorant attempt to ridicule the Americans, and it always turns out that their greatest blunder and greatest crime consists in not sending their cotton to England and in not taking England's manufactures. Until of late I had lived under the impression that the Americans had a deal to answer for in cherishing a bad feeling towards England, which was entirely unjustified by the disposition of the English people towards them; but a worse spirit than anything I have ever read of in America is constantly displaying itself among the factory squires and shopocrats of England, while the sympathies of the aristocracy are undisguisedly offered to the rebellious Southerners. And it is remarkable how little original thought appears to be expended on this fratricidal war. Liberal journalists and popular lecturers repeat each other without end; but no one thinks it worth his while to investigate the causes of the quarrel with earnestness, and place the whole case before the public in the light which the history of the last five-and-twenty years might throw upon it."

Looking at the faded old colonial newspaper on which these words appear, how vividly one realises that there was something more than mere empty compliment in the felicitous phrases of the Mayor of New York, who, in congratulating the Queen on her Jubilee, recalled the fact that it was largely through the personal influence of herself and the Prince Consort that England had not thrown herself into this great struggle on the side of the South. One must also pay a tribute to the masculine common-sense of Sir Henry Parkes, who not only declined to go with the stream, but did not suffer his judgment to be distorted by the two Englishmen, for whom, in literature and politics, he then felt supreme admiration—I allude to Thomas Carlyle and Mr.

Gladstone.[1] As we all know, the dire catastrophe of a war between Great Britain and America was almost precipitated by the seizure of Slidell and Mason by the United States frigate *San Jacinto* from off the British ship *Trent*. Sir Henry Parkes' letter, dated December 24th, 1861, was written just as this startling news was brought to Southampton. In the same budget he bewails the death of the Prince Consort, and in plain words, not devoid of pathos, depicts the effect of these tidings on the people of England.

"This will be a solemn Christmas Eve in England. Thousands of artisan families will meet it with the bitter prospect of want and starvation blanching their cheeks, and very many of their employers will hardly be able to turn their gaze from the brink of ruin on which they stand to the objects of grief and apprehension which weigh down the public mind. Breaking through the commercial gloom, every hour and from every quarter, have come of late the discordant notes of warlike preparation, and the heavy tolling of the bell of death. Never, perhaps, was the nation in a more sorrowful mood, and never had it deeper cause for sorrow. Let us reason as we will, we cannot free ourselves

---

[1] See Mr. Hurlbert's severe censure of Mr. Gladstone:— *Ireland under Coercion*, Prologue p. xxix.

from the painful consciousness that we are about to plunge into a fratricidal war—about to vindicate our honour in the shadow of the blood-red banners of slavery. Bold and boastful as is the language of the London Press, it is easy to see that there is a tremor in the writer's hand. Every second morning a tone of misgiving seems to soften the reckless bravery of the *Times*. It will not do; people cannot satisfy their consciences, though goaded on by the sense of insult, that it is a high Christian thing to burden the nation with debt, and to spill the nation's blood on the wrong side of the American civil broils. At first the sense of wrong sent every man's hand to the sword-hilt. But the hard logic of consequences has tempered men's minds wonderfully during the last three weeks. Those who are little affected by feelings of brotherhood, or sympathy with freedom, see reason to pause in the loss of trade and the increase of taxation, and I doubt much whether if war be declared it will long remain a popular war."

This letter, we must bear in mind, was being penned at the time when the British Cabinet were hastily summoned to consider the affair of the *Trent*. The writer was fully aware that a Privy Council, attended by the Queen, was held at Windsor three days after the news of the seizure of Slidell and Mason had reached England, and that, on the same day, a Queen's Messenger left London with a despatch for Lord Lyons. Above all, he was not likely to forget that Lord Palmerston was the Prime Minister. To the eyes of the Australian, indeed, war seemed imminent. He weighed the *pros* and *cons* with a judicial hand. But on the whole he evidently came to the conclusion that the war party would carry the day, unless the two men, taken from the deck of a British ship, were given up to the British Ambassador. The whole affair, as we know, passed away like a summer cloud; the two Southerners were surrendered by the American Government to Lord Lyons, and duly resumed, on board the war-ship *Rinaldo*, their voyage to England, where their mission ended in failure. But the words of Sir Henry Parkes must have made a profound impression in Sydney a quarter of a century ago; for, be it remembered, this was before the era of the submarine cable, and the anxious colonists had to wait a month, sitting as it were in outer darkness, between each flash of intelligence, knowing not what fate was in store either for the mother country or themselves.

On that "solemn Christmas Eve" Sir Henry did not close his budget without giving his fellow-colonists a timely warning. In emphatic words he pointed out that the British statesmen and journalists, who were so loudly clamouring for war with America, took no heed whatever of the defenceless condition of the Australian colonies. He could only charitably think that the sudden appearance of Yankee armed cruisers in the waters of Port Jackson and Hobson's Bay had never even been dreamt of by these bellicose Englishmen; but he added:—

"You may depend upon it that if England and America plunge into a great naval war, American privateering will exceed anything of the kind known of other countries in former times. There are thousands of men who sail under the stars and stripes who possess the adventurous spirit and desperate courage which fit the privateer for his peculiar kind of aggressive operations in a naval war. You had better lose no time in preparing for your defence. Do not lull yourselves into a false sense of security by depending too much upon the naval superiority of England. . . . Sydney and the surrounding district ought to muster five thousand volunteers."

In the same letter Sir Henry records, not without

pathos, the death of Prince Albert. All that he says concerning the bereaved Queen and her departed consort is in excellent taste, but I prefer to present his stray comments on the men and events that fell more directly under his own searching eyes. In a letter dated February 28, 1862, he gives a full account of the opening of Parliament, and makes some interesting remarks on the great and little parliamentarians of the day. His description of Disraeli's speech, considering the writer's pronounced Liberal proclivities, is certainly conceived in a generous spirit. After disposing of its earlier portion, with the dubious compliment that "no man could have contrived to say nothing with more adroitness or more show of profundity," he pays this high tribute to its closing eloquence :—

"With faltering voice he passed on to the great sorrow of the nation, and as he took up his new subject the true orator appeared. His voice scarcely rose above a mournful whisper—so tremulous with feeling and yet so clear—and his words were of the simplest and fittest as he spoke of the true worth of the departed Prince, and of the immeasurable greatness of the nation's loss. Every breath communicated its pathetic tones to every heart among his listeners as he recounted the many virtues that survived to perpetuate the memory of the dead ; and when he had concluded with a soul-touching allusion to the grief of the Queen, one felt that the strain of eloquence which had just ceased was of that order which could never be given to others in written words."

Of Lord Palmerston's speech in reply to Mr. Disraeli, the Australian parliamentarian is somewhat contemptuous. "Your Mr. Cowper," he observes, with an adroit hit at a very capable rival Sydney politician, "might have said all that the Prime Minister of England said, and said it with quite as much oratorical effect. But there was this difference between Lord Palmerston's commonplaces and Mr. Cowper's: the old English Minister knew exactly the limits within which he must confine himself, and seemed perfectly to know the temper of his audience and the state of feeling outside."

The minor lights that attempted to shine that evening, notably Sir Robert Peel (Sir Robert *fils*, of course), struck him as beneath contempt.

On a subsequent evening he attended the House of Commons in order to hear a debate of special interest to himself and his colonial readers. It was the debate raised by Mr. Arthur Mills, then member for Taunton, on the question of Colonial defences. At this time Professor Goldwin Smith was raising the great controversy as to the mutual benefits that would flow from England's recognising the complete independence of her self-governing colonies. The discussion in Parliament was devoted to the minor point of the advisability of withdrawing English troops from these dependencies. Sir Henry confesses himself little edified, and was compelled to beguile the tedium by counting the House, which, however, was an easy task, for, "including Mr. Childers," there were only twenty-seven present. All the time, he tells us, he was on the *qui vive* to hear the once famous author of *Sam Slick*, " with his Nova-Scotian instincts," on this Colonial question; but when Haliburton rose "he said just nothing, and that nothing in as uninteresting a way as any other old gentleman with a portly figure and well-used countenance could well adopt."

It is characteristic that Sir Henry Parkes devotes little of his correspondence to the great Exhibition of 1862. As a newspaper correspondent for the time being, he recognises his remissness, saying that he was never fond of running with the crowd, but that when the "Japanese Ambassadors and Honourables from the Antipodes" have stared at everything to their fill, then he may go to South Kensington. In the meantime, he travels about from town to town, at one time seeing the widowed Queen pass through Stafford on her way to the Highlands, at another, encountering Prince Arthur, "a fine little boy of twelve," at Gloucester. In his general survey of the social condition of England he seems to have been much struck by the large and increasing number of societies among the working classes for their self-improvement. Next to this, he notices the movement for extending the sphere of employment among women, and singles out Miss Emily Faithfull as its leading pioneer. Among politicians he seems to have conceived a special affection for Cobden, chiefly, I think, because he had sprung from the ranks. "No man," he writes, "has more of that inspiring simplicity of manner, and that calm, almost spiritual, earnestness of purpose, which, combined with comprehensive thought and the patient power of labour, are sure to gain the moral mastery. In his case these qualities illuminate enduring public services and a reputation already historical."

It is curious to notice that twenty-five years ago this Australian in England should ask who is to govern the country half a dozen years hence. "The old statesmen are dying off. The next six years will make terrible havoc with the names that have been most familiar to the ears of the last two generations. As they descend into the valley of shadows, where are the men of calm strength and vigour coming up the other side of the hill bearing the standard of either party?" He prophesied that if the hand of death should spare them, Cobden, Gladstone, and Stanley would combine and govern England. Clearly, with all his ability, Sir Henry had not the gift of prophecy; and little did it occur to him that he would live to see Bright and Gladstone marshalling opposing forces, and both still swaying vast multitudes of their countrymen in this year of grace 1888.

One of the most pathetic incidents recorded in these letters is that of Lord Brougham's inaugural address to the Social Science Congress, delivered at Exeter Hall on June 5th, 1862. It is rather painful reading, but my sketch would be incomplete without it:—

"I had never heard Lord Brougham speak, and

was very anxious to listen to that voice, of the force and vehemence of which I had heard such glowing descriptions. Accordingly, I got to Exeter Hall full three-quarters of an hour before the time of meeting, and selected my own position in a line with the chair, and not more than five seats from the platform. It was considerably past the appointed time when the statesman-philosopher made his appearance amidst a burst of hearty and grateful cheers. He walked along the front of the platform with bowed head and tottering step, never raising his eyes, and he took his seat with evident difficulty. After some preliminaries he rose slowly, and with a painful effort, and commenced reading his address from manuscript. His voice was so harsh and indistinct that I could not hear one word in three throughout the delivery, and the exertion necessary for this was so severely felt that he was compelled to resume his seat before many leaves were turned over. In asking for this indulgence, he spoke in what appeared to me a tone of mortified pride, and with a manner so confused that the meeting did not instantly comprehend his meaning. When the sad meaning flashed upon them, every person present seemed to join in a burst of assenting sympathising cheers. But the illustrious Brougham is not the man of iron frame which his admirers have represented him to be, and which it would accord with our feeling of wonder at his prodigious labours in times past to believe him to be. A careful reading of the address he delivered on this occasion will, I fear, lead to the conclusion that his noble intellect is also giving way. Its style for the most part is coarse and declamatory, while nothing could be more inconsequential than some of its reasonings."

Sir Henry saw Lord Brougham on two subsequent occasions; once when he was conducted by Dr. Travers Twiss and M. Garnier Pagès into the room at Burlington House set apart for the International Law Section of the Congress. On that occasion M. Garnier Pagès, we are told, delivered an animated speech in favour of International Law Reform, which roused Lord Brougham to express his admiration of the "extraordinary eloquence" of the French orator, who was formerly "one of the seven Kings of France." A few nights after this, Lord Brougham officiating with Lord Shaftesbury and others as the hosts, received some three or four thousand guests at the Social Science Soirée at the Palace of Westminster. "I saw him," writes Sir Henry, "as late as eleven o'clock in conversation with the aged poet, Dean Milman, and, notwithstanding the fatigues he had undergone, he looked much fresher than at Exeter Hall."

Our Australian in England gladly availed himself of an opportunity to witness the ceremony of conferring the D.C.L. at Oxford upon Lord Palmerston and other distinguished men, on July 2d, 1862. Sir Henry seems to have been somewhat disgusted with the horse-play of the undergraduates, but what distressed him most was their enthusiasm on behalf of the Southern States.

"The name of Disraeli brought down a thundering cheer, but Jeff Davis and the Southern States were responded to still louder; Mr. Gladstone, though the University's own member, was not cheered." In addition to Lord Palmerston, Sir James Outram, Sir Roundell Palmer, Professor Wheatstone, and Henry Taylor, were to receive the D.C.L.

"The names of Palmerston and Outram were enthusiastically and repeatedly cheered, but the others did not appear to be objects of special favour. . . . The announcement of Henry Taylor's name was followed by the not very complimentary inquiry, 'Who is he?' I felt myself somewhat honoured by being permitted to inform a veritable Master of Arts that Henry Taylor was the author of *Philip Van Artevelde*. I think I never saw so glorious-looking a man as Henry Taylor. His head is large and finely formed, with massy silvery hair, a long waving lock in front being quite golden. His forehead is broad and lofty, his eyes full, his cheeks inclining to florid. The lower part of his face is covered by a long flowing beard, which singularly befits his noble countenance, beaming with an expression of mingled power and benevolence."

Who can forget Sir Henry Taylor's own account of Lord Palmerston's behaviour on this occasion, when Professor Wheatstone expounded to him the wonders of Telegraphy? "The man of science was slow, the man of the world *seemed* attentive; the man of science was copious, the man of the world let nothing escape him; the man of science unfolded the anticipated results—another and another, the man of the world listened with all his ears; and I was saying to myself, his patience is exemplary, but will it last for ever? When I heard the issue—'God bless my soul, you don't say so!

I *must* get you to tell that to the Lord Chancellor!' And the man of the world took the man of science to another part of the room, hooked him on to Lord Westbury, and bounded away like a horse let loose in a pasture."

The Australian " Sir Henry " was not privileged to witness this scene, but how he would have enjoyed it! Lord Palmerston's irresistible jauntiness, however, made its due impression upon him. " As he brushed past where I was standing, I could not help admiring the animal spirits mantling his cheeks—more like the glow of youth than the complexion of fourscore years. He was visibly moved by his reception. I saw him later in the day driving through Oxford in his red gown, and he seemed as hilarious as a boy of fifteen."

It is curious, and even affecting, to notice how lovingly this world-worn colonist and man of affairs regarded English rural sights and sounds, after an absence from them of twenty years. His final letter, indeed, is entirely devoted to them, and is headed " Rural England and the Railways." He tells his readers that when he emigrated to Australia there were only two railways in operation in England, and he feared that their extension might have defaced and driven away the sweet familiar sights and sounds of English country life. To his great delight he found this to be a delusion. He notices how familiar the partridges, and the wild creatures of the field and copse, have become with the flaming iron-horse, so that they "seldom leave their haunts, or quicken their pace, at his coming." So he found it with pheasant, fox, and hare. "The railway team is the same to them as the winds and the lightnings."

"And the flowers," he bursts out, "the sweet familiar flowers of an English spring! They have seized upon the railways as part of their rightful heritage. In all directions the deep slopes, where the railway spans some valley, are thickly starred with the pale primrose, and the maidenly cowslips nod to the passengers from the brows of the cutting through the gentle hills. . . . The railways do no more than run their fine lines through the rural landscape, making sunny banks for the flowers and shrubs most loved by the English people. Though places which have a name in history are undoubtedly visited by a larger number than formerly, I am inclined to think there are many nooks and corners of rural England which are more secluded from the world now than when the world's travellers had to journey by the common road."

With a personal apology to Mr. Ruskin, we must here part with the distinguished Australian, who surely in fancy was for a while once again a Warwickshire lad.

I have had a purpose in view in emphasising Sir Henry Parkes' impressions of English public opinion at the time of the American Civil War. Some of the quotations from his letters that I have given—and there is much more and even stronger writing to be found in the originals—might well have been supposed to emanate from the indignant pen of some itinerant New-Englander. Yet Sir Henry Parkes knew no country but England up to the time of his early manhood, and since then his career has formed a part of the history of a great English colony.

To my mind, the passing impressions of such an Australian in England are of intrinsic historic value. Being removed from the unconscious partiality even of the cultured Englishman, and free from the unsympathetic superciliousness of the "intelligent foreigner," they are allied to the impartial judgments of posterity. Viewed in this light the sympathetic comprehension displayed by the Australian politician towards America is perhaps a fore-glimpse of the time when the various communities of the Old and the New Worlds, which speak the English tongue, and are mainly of English race, shall, under whatever number of local governments, be as one people and as one nation.

CHAPTER III.

LORD BEACONSFIELD AND YOUNG AUSTRALIA.

In recently overhauling a chaotic accumulation of colonial books, pamphlets, and political documents, I lighted upon a suggestive out-of-the-way chapter in the brief annals of "Young Australia," which, I think, should not be suffered to pass without the tribute of an ephemeral sketch. It seems to me that the mere fact of Lord Beaconsfield exercising so potent a fascination on a number of young men born, or at least bred, in our remote antipodean colonies, alone gives to my reminiscence an element of some general interest. Australia is now in direct hourly communication with the Motherland by means of the magic submarine cable, and nothing transpires of importance from day to day without its being known within twenty-four hours in the far-off Island Continent. Lord Carnarvon asserts that recently, when in Melbourne and

Sydney, he could follow the variations of "home" politics almost as well as if he had been in London. But my readers may remember that when the cable broke, some little time ago, the Victorian Government utilised the misfortune by an experimental mobilisation of their naval and military forces. They wisely wanted to test how they would have been placed if the breakage had been the work of a hostile power. Yet so quickly do we grow accustomed to the miracles of science, and take them as ordinary matters of course, that Australians require such temporary interruptions of telegraphic communication to realise the time when they knew what was going on in Europe only by means of the monthly mail steamer. It was not so long ago, yet it seems like another era—like the division between ancient and modern colonial history. We were in this condition of all but outer darkness, when the great struggle between France and Germany was fought out. Just picture the excitement when the English mails came in bearing their burden of accumulated news! On August 22, 1872, Mr. Charles Todd, Postmaster-General of South Australia, announced that we were in telegraphic communication with England. When, therefore, the next

European convulsion occurred—the Russo-Turkish War—we experienced the unwonted excitement of following the campaign from day to day. It was a time of intense excitement in our remote regions. To us, as to most Englishmen, since the Crimean War, Russia, with her Asiatic armies and North Pacific squadron, loomed as the natural enemy of the British Empire.[1] For years past, to such a pitch of overwrought excitement had we brought ourselves, that rarely did a Russian cruiser enter one of our harbours, but we attributed the visit to some deep-laid treacherous design. The unwelcome visitor had come in order to take soundings, to map down the position of our ineffective defences, and to note where his shells would most effectively burst in our streets. I am not justifying, but merely recording, what may often have been most unwarranted, and perhaps ignoble, suspicions. But this being the prevailing colonial sentiment with regard to Russia, it is not difficult to imagine how eagerly we followed the struggle between Muscovite and Mussul-

[1] I have lived long enough to think that this is the greatest condemnation of the policy of that war into which we were mainly led by the restless artifices of Napoleon III., who also by his timidity prevented us from reaping any advantages from our nominal success.

man, and the varying European complications resulting therefrom. Thus it was that Disraeli, whose career had always possessed for many cultured young Australians the glamour of a strange fascination, suddenly began to loom from out the mist of English party politics, as the great patriotic statesman of the English-speaking world. Plain prose was found at times inadequate to the expression of our admiration, and "patriotic sonneteering" in honour of Beaconsfield was not unknown among us. But the ablest of these political young Australians eschewed the tinklings of verse, preferring to compose weighty articles on "the Political Future of Europe," and to plead for Colonial representation in the so-called Imperial Parliament.

The verses, though inferior in political grasp and intellectual ability, serve best to show the fervour with which "Young Australia" regarded the wonderful man who was then guiding the helm of State. I transcribe from the *Melbourne Review*, where they originally appeared, two Sonnets, which, so lasting has been my admiration for Lord Beaconsfield, I do not altogether blush to own, after the cooling lapse of years :—

ENGLAND, 1877.

Thou hast not played the braggart in our time,
    O land of Commerce, foremost once in War!
    Among the guardians of thy sacred shore
Are those who preach to all that War is crime,
"Sweet peace," they cry, "should reign from clime
    to clime."
    But look abroad! The Cossack wades through
    gore
To stretch his wide dominions more and more,
Muttering his prayers, meantime, like some base
    mime.
While, as of old, O glorious Mother Isle!
    Thou hast arrayed thyself in warlike might,
    Waiting expectant to uphold the right.
Thy battle-ships are at the envied gates;
And thy brief words in scorn of Russia's guile
    Have won respect from cold and alien States.

MELBOURNE, *September* 1877.

The second Sonnet was even more bellicose; for it was composed on receipt of the stirring intelligence that Indian troops had been despatched to Malta.

ENGLAND, 1878.

Before the nations once again she stands
   In all the glory of pre-eminence!
   Her mighty Empire, with its millions dense,
Spread o'er the earth in far divided lands,
Yet all resolved to do her stern commands—
   Like Rome, in her world-wide magnificence.
Shall she then brook the Russian's dire offence,
Nor strive to stay his fell remorseless hands?
   Let other powers watch in impotence,
Our England shall not basely stand aside,
   While the despoiler robs his hapless prey:
Her armoured ships in Moslem waters ride,
   Her swarthy Sepoys swarm in war's array;
And English hearts throb strong with patriot pride.

   MELBOURNE, *August* 1878.

After the result of the Berlin Congress was declared, it was felt that the hour had come when Australia should testify to her sense of the worth and patriotism of Lord Beaconsfield. So far as Melbourne was concerned, this idea originated with the knot of enthusiastic young Australians to whom I have referred. But it would have been impossible to organise a vast public meeting such as that which took place at the Melbourne Town-hall on

July 29, 1878, "to express public appreciation of the services of the Earl of Beaconsfield in the settlement of the Eastern Question," unless there had been a very large amount of public sentiment in support of it. This was undoubtedly the case. Nearly every grown man in the place was an admirer of Lord Beaconsfield, the only exceptions being those who had no patriotic feeling, and were too utterly stupid to have any opinions on Imperial politics, and those "cranks" (to use an admirable American term) whose cleverness furnishes them with paradoxical reasons for differing with their fellow-creatures. Such being the condition of the public mind, it was not difficult to organise a Beaconsfield demonstration in Melbourne. The necessary preliminary formalities having been observed, the Mayor called a public meeting, which, although held in the afternoon, was attended by some 3000 persons, and the two chief speakers had both been Premiers of the colony. The *Melbourne Argus* was quite justified in asserting that it was "one of the most interesting and enthusiastic that Melbourne has ever witnessed." The speech of Mr. James Service,[1] the ex-Premier of Victoria (who won

---

[1] See Appendix F, "A Typical Australian Statesman."

golden opinions from English statesmen as one of the Victorian delegates at the Colonial Conference held at Downing Street last year), in praise of the extraordinary man who had brought us "Peace with Honour," was worthy of a great occasion. With thorough personal conviction, and that power of restrained enthusiasm so effective with an Australian as well as with an English audience, Mr. Service impressed upon that huge Melbourne meeting that it was entirely "through the energy, the judgment, the resolution, and the still strong power manifested by Lord Beaconsfield that we have secured for ourselves the blessings of peace, and that we have secured those blessings without an imputation upon the honour of England." It is not necessary to dwell on the rest of the proceedings further than to say that the oratory of the lesser lights was equally enthusiastic; but it is worthy of special note that by far the most able and eloquent of Mr. Service's supporters on this occasion was Mr. David Gaunson, who was then the leading young Native Victorian politician. Mr. Gaunson fairly aroused the enthusiasm of that monster colonial gathering by what used to be nick-named in England "Jingoism." The meeting unanimously decided that the

Governor of the colony should be requested to transmit the principal resolution by telegraph to the Earl of Beaconsfield; and an illuminated Address was fitly prepared and forwarded by the outgoing mail. Nor did Melbourne stand alone. Throughout the length and breadth of Australia the name of Benjamin Disraeli, Earl of Beaconsfield, made the sunburnt settler glow with an unwonted pride of patriotism. A similar meeting to our Melbourne one was held in Sydney, while the two municipal councils of Ballarat—commercially the second city of Victoria, with a political vigour and activity second to none in Australia—sent congratulatory telegrams to the great English statesman. Adelaide, the metropolis of South Australia, and Newcastle, the second city in New South Wales, helped to swell this pæan of truly Imperial praise.

In an admirable leading article which appeared in the *Melbourne Argus*, the writer aptly observed: "The veteran statesman can scarcely fail to experience a lively sense of satisfaction in finding that the courage and wisdom of his conduct have met with the cordial approbation of his countrymen at the Antipodes; for we are so far removed from the influences which disturb men's views and warp their judgments upon questions of foreign policy in the mother country, that the opinions expressed here and in Sydney resemble, in some respects, the verdict of history, both in its impartiality and its deliberateness." Lord Beaconsfield duly acknowledged our patriotic tributes in the customary way, but, perhaps, we shall some day know how he was really affected by this singular outburst of personal, not less than public, admiration from outlying dependencies of the Empire, the like of which no other English statesman has ever evoked. It may be worth inquiring why this is so. If we consider the elements out of which an Australian colony is mainly composed, we find hardly anything analogous to the old Tory party in Church and State of which Disraeli became the leader—and educator—in this country. A colony is simply composed of a vigorous, wage-earning, or working class, and an equally hard-working, though more wealthy, employer or professional class, the latter corresponding to the "middle class" in Great Britain. In other words, there are no landed gentry, no aristocracy, and no "leisured class." If we consider such a community as that of Victoria, we shall find that the preponderating majority of the more earnest-minded men—that is, of those who have the making of political leaders and influential citizens—carried with them from the mother country strong working-class or middle-class opinions and prejudices. What could be more alien to such people than much of the political philosophy of Disraeli's novels? Yet it is a fatal mistake for the ordinary English Liberal or Radical to assert that we democratic colonists were simply fascinated and deluded by Lord Beaconsfield's "showy foreign policy," and what they used to term his "sham Imperialism." It is doubtless the want of all Imperial sentiment, which has marked the English Liberals under the long papacy of Mr. Gladstone, that in the first instance alienated the colonists from a leader whose genius works most smoothly on the broad but perilous path of political disintegration.[1] Nothing

[1] A much-esteemed friend deprecates this harsh criticism of Mr. Gladstone, and quotes the Rev. Dr. West, "the revered Vicar of St. Mary Magdalene, Paddington," to the effect that the Liberal Premier bestowed his Church patronage wisely; my correspondent adding, "like a loyal Churchman and true Statesman," whereas "Mr. Disraeli's appointments were purely on political or personal grounds." I am, however, not dealing with Mr. Gladstone as an English Churchman, but as an English Statesman. Even in the former capacity I do not see that he has exhibited a distressing loyalty to his religious ideals; nor will his name be linked with any measure of ecclesiastical policy except the disestablishment of the Church of Ireland. This may have been a necessary, but it was an iconoclastic act.

is so distasteful to loyal colonists as the idea that Britain would voluntarily abdicate her pride of place among the nations. Their reading of history convinces them that they are in peaceful possession of their vast island-continent, simply because Nelson and Wellington defeated and overwhelmed the navies and armies of Napoleon. And in this light Lord Beaconsfield seemed a worthier successor of Pitt than Mr. Gladstone. But even beyond this they judged this remarkable man more correctly than the mass of his countryman at "home," more, as the Colonial editor remarked, with the "impartiality and deliberateness of posterity." At all events, whatever may be the cause, these so-called democratic colonies felt a much greater admiration for, and a much stronger personal interest in, Lord Beaconsfield towards the close of his wonderful career than ever they have felt for his distinguished opponent. The colonial newspaper from which I have already quoted went on to say: "These meetings will also convince the Earl of Beaconsfield and his colleagues of the strength of the Imperial sentiment, even in the most distant portions of the Empire, and will help, we hope, to invigorate the feeling in England in favour of a closer union between all its members, and of the transformation of Great into Greater Britain."

These words were written more than ten years ago. How far have we travelled the Imperial highway then pointed out? Not far, I fear. Since then the Australian colonists have had frequent opportunities of gauging the political aims and aspirations of Mr. Gladstone as head of the State, with the inevitable result of deepening their admiration of Lord Beaconsfield. The foreign and domestic policy of Great Britain since 1880 has been more minutely submitted to colonial critics, thanks to the cable, than was ever before possible. As a result, nowhere is Mr. Gladstone so completely discarded as in Australia and New Zealand. The crowning disgrace—as the majority of colonists regard it—was, of course, his Irish Home Rule Bill. If anything could have destroyed their loyalty, and made them despair of the Empire, it was this deplorable measure of disintegration.

CHAPTER IV.

AUSTRALIAN DEMOCRACY.

IF a fresh De Tocqueville could arise, and were to make a wide excursion to the Antipodes, he would find ample material for a new work on "Democracy in Australia," or rather, in "Australasia,"—for the adjacent islands of New Zealand would furnish a most important section. The political philosopher on his travels would encounter seven self-governing democratic States, all claiming to be members of a world-wide empire whose nucleus is a Constitutional Monarchy with an hereditary House of Peers. To such a mind these British colonies would present a series of problems of surpassing fascination; problems which can barely be stated, much less discussed, in a brief chapter, the object of which is simply to explain the ascendency of the democratic form of government in Australia.

And here, at the outset, I would remark that in my opinion the painstaking labours of more than one colonial historian have been entirely wasted by reason of an unconquerable anti-democratic bias. One need not go quite so far as that worthy old Victorian colonist who stoutly maintained that no one who did not firmly believe in democratic institutions had any right to live in Australia. Such a law would promote a very considerable exodus. But assuredly it seems to me that no one can be trusted to relate the annals, or trace the social and political evolution of Australia, who starts with an invincible prejudice against democracies. It is to be regretted that such writers, when they expatiate pungently on the degradation of their countrymen, whether of republican America or of self-governing democratic Australia, receive a too-ready and sympathetic hearing in England. Yet what would be thought if Mr. Henry Labouchere were accepted by our non-aristocratic kinsmen across the seas as the final and most philosophic authority on such an institution as the House of Lords?

It was inevitable that the Australians, as soon as the matter was placed in their own hands, would frame their political institutions on a democratic pattern. No doubt the greatest of Australian statesmen thought, or at least hoped, that it might be otherwise. While paying the largest tribute to the genius of Wentworth, it must be said that on this point he was grievously in error. Yet if such a man, with such commanding talents and so splendid a record of past services, utterly failed to create a patrician element in colonial society, what hope could there be save in the frank acceptance of democratic institutions? Wentworth's idea in brief was to make Australia a *replica* of England rather than of America. To effect this he boldly proposed, as a part of his Constitution Bill, the creation of a colonial House of Peers. His views on this question were not lightly formed.

He knew the curious elements out of which the new nation was to be evolved better than any other man. For years he had fought for the rights and liberties of the people, and throughout his whole life the love of his native country, Australia, was to him a passion. But his imperial instincts were likewise great, and in the full maturity of his splendid powers he could see no way of creating a free self-governed Australia, worthy of an ultimate partnership with the mother-country, without establishing, along with colonial autonomy, a colonial aristocracy. The subject had been for years maturing in his mind; he even expounded his views on this question of an Australian House of Lords in a long-forgotten article in the pages of an English magazine. Nothing can surpass the full tide of his eloquence, when on these momentous themes he essayed to address his fellow-colonists in Sydney, many of whom, even in his lifetime, had come to regard him as the Washington of the Antipodes. Yet on this point of creating a brand-new colonial aristocracy he failed miserably. The commonest street orator in Sydney could raise a ready laugh by giving a list of the expectant "nobility." Robert Lowe opposed it in the House of Commons, and his criticism had all the weight of his "colonial experience"; while a "young Sydney tradesman, by name Henry Parkes," as Dr. Lang described the present Premier of New South Wales, first rose into public notoriety and favour by his diatribes against this feature of Wentworth's great measure. Despite the unrivalled weight of Wentworth's personal ascendency, his notion of "manufacturing" a privileged order was all but unanimously scouted, even in a colony that had been dry-nursed by Imperial officialdom and dragooned by military martinets. What chance then would it have had among the miners, artisans, and farmers of Victoria?

It cannot be doubted that in the latter colony, then newly born, there must have been many who watched Wentworth's daring experiment with eager expectancy, and a kind of despairing hope that it might succeed. Like the officials of the older dependency, they dreaded the plunge into the democratic cold-bath which they felt awaited them the moment the Imperial Government withdrew its guiding hand. Yet it is only fair to them to say that they put a brave face on the matter. As soon as the system of responsible government was inaugurated, there was a rapid quickening of the democratic pace. In an incredibly short space of time the local House of Commons in each of the colonies was elected by manhood suffrage and the ballot. Constitutional changes in a popular direction were made almost with a colony's birth. In Victoria, hardly had the first Ministry under responsible government fairly got into their seats, when Mr. William Nicholson, a quiet, respectable, private member, carried against them a motion in favour of vote by ballot, which almost immediately became the law of the land, and from the first has worked admirably. It is amusing to notice how anxious Dr. Lang is to claim the credit of any and every possible kind of reform inaugurated during his fifty years of political activity in Australia. Unfortunately he knew little or nothing of Mr. Nicholson, but he consoled himself with the reflection that the Victorian legislator must have acquired his notions about the ballot from a former literary assistant of his, who was then Town-Clerk of Melbourne. In this way, to the great satisfaction of the majority, but the evident alarm of not a few, did the colonists *democratise* their Constitutions. Hard and bitter were the recriminations of both parties during the brief but determined struggle.

It is a very difficult matter to review what is all but contemporary colonial history in an impartial spirit. For my part, I do not attempt to conceal my popular sympathies; but this does not imply surely that I should be prepared to justify every act of the popular party in these heterogeneous democratic colonies. Yet this is the assumption that runs through every page of a work like Mr. G. W. Rusden's *History of Australia*. Government is at

AUSTRALIAN DEMOCRACY 83

best a rude human contrivance, but the justification of colonial democracy broadly rests on the fact that the colonies could not be governed in accordance with their progressive needs either from Downing Street or by Colonial Office nominees located in the colonies. That being granted, and as a consequence "responsible government" established, there was no possible halfway-house between an irresponsible bureaucratic system and open and avowed democracy.

But the real secret of the rapid triumph of democratic principles was simply this: the party opposed to them was in the truest sense of the term the *anti-colonial* party. In the early stages of these colonies the members of this party regarded their stay in these immature communities simply as a kind of exile. When they had amassed sufficient money they intended to retire and live in England. With all their gentlemanly characteristics and fine manly virtues, this was the case with a great majority of those splendid pioneer squatters of Port Phillip, now Victoria. With the heterogeneous influx of population, caused by the gold-fields, the aristocratic disgust of these men towards the colony was intensified. It therefore happened by a process of natural selection that the democratic party became identical with the colonial, or locally patriotic party; and of course when the conflict came it was victorious all along the line. I am endeavouring at every turn to keep clear of the petty details of party polemics in Australia, and the English reader will be good enough to believe that in refraining from illustrating my points by manifold examples, I do so mainly in his interest. If, however, he will bear in mind that democracy in this way came to be allied in the colonial mind with local patriotism, with a belief in the excellence and in the future of Australia as a land which a man might fitly regard as the *patria* of his race, he will readily understand its rapid triumph.

At the same time, this generalisation is somewhat too sweeping. As we have seen, the greatest of Australian public men, and one who certainly was filled with Australian patriotism, favoured the formation of aristocratic, rather than democratic, institutions, for his own particular colony, New South Wales. Sir William Foster Stawell, whose Australian patriotism is quite as strong as Wentworth's, would have probably preferred an anti-democratic constitution for Victoria.

But these really great colonial anti-democrats were, after all, on this vital point of local patriotism, by no means typical of their class. The self-styled "upper classes" of Australia for many years (and the feeling is hardly yet dead) regarded their residence at the Antipodes, as I have already remarked, as a kind of exile. From this state of things arose what may be termed the optimism of the democratic leaders, grounded as it was in their firm faith in Australia as a permanent home for themselves and their descendants, and the equally marked, but fatal pessimism of the colonial "upper-class" party. Turning over the Victorian *Hansard* from 1865 onward, one must be struck with this essential difference in the *tone* of the two parties. It is often noticeable that the opposing disputants are very fairly matched, but one feels in reviewing these debates that the men who proclaimed their belief in the colony deserved to prevail over those who decried it.

On this particular point I was much impressed recently by reading a debate on a motion introduced on May 20th, 1869, by the present Judge Casey of Victoria, proposing to refer certain privileges of the Legislative Assembly to the decision of the

Privy Council.[1] It was an especially unpleasant case, but in reading this suggestive debate, one may see how vigorously a democracy, through its leaders, may assert both its rights and its public conscience.

Two members of the Legislative Assembly had been convicted of receiving bribes, and were expelled; more than this the two *bribers*, who had behind them all the weight and respectability of local "squatterdom," were committed to prison, but released by the Supreme Court. This was the point in dispute, and the lawyer who opposed the popular party in thus bringing to punishment the corrupters, as well as the corrupted, made out from a purely legal point of view a very good case. But no one whose own life and future were at all bound up in that of Victoria but must have felt the irresistible force of every word used by

---

[1] The attitude of Mr. Higinbotham in this matter is not to be taken as in any way hostile to the Judicial Committee of the Privy Council as a final Court of Appeal. Perhaps that Committee might be strengthened by the accession of really eminent Colonial legists, such as Judge Molesworth of Victoria, but its decisions have ever been received with universal confidence and respect in Australia. Mr. Higinbotham's contention in this debate was that the local Supreme Court had no power to over-ride the decision of the local Legislature, on a matter affecting its own rights and privileges.

the popular democratic leader, Mr. Higinbotham (now Chief-Justice of the colony), in reply. He said :—

"Of course all depends on whether the mass of the population really desire honesty in public affairs, and will support their representatives in endeavouring to secure it, or whether they are prepared to desert us, and will, in deserting us, prove, as I think the honourable and learned member for St. Kilda has said, that politics and politicians, and all men in this country, are rotten to the core. I am willing to stand on that issue. If the people of this country will not support us in our endeavours to purify Parliament and to maintain the authority of Parliament, why then, sir, let corruption be established, and let every man who respects himself retire from public life. I have only one more word to say. I have faith in the honesty and integrity of the mass of the people of this country. I believe they will support us in our endeavours, and relying on that support—and until that support is withdrawn—I am prepared to take steps against both the bribed and the bribers, such as shall, if possible, correct the erring judgment of constituencies, and shall give a most certain and convincing proof to all persons, including the judges of the land, who interfere with our rights, that we have the power as well as the right to assert and enforce our rights, and in doing so to perform our duty."—(*Victorian Hansard*, vii. p. 783-8.)

Quite apart from the Constitutional question in debate, it will be noticed that, while the anti-democratic leader plainly avowed his pessimistic disbelief in the soundness of the body politic, the popular orator much more earnestly proclaimed his faith, as a basis for all legislative action, in the integrity of his fellow-colonists. These claims on behalf of the colonial democracy, based on its patriotism and public spirit, may even at this late day be met by the kind of cheap abuse that was once so common in the English press. Even so clever a man as Mr. Harold Finch-Hatton[1] seems to think that he is dealing with colonial politics in a sparkling and yet strictly impartial spirit, when he has related two or three stale derogatory stories against sundry local demagogues. The worst of it is, he imagines that these stray crumbs of club scandal are quite sufficient to overwhelm the entire political

---

[1] See *Advance Australia!* by the Hon. Harold Finch-Hatton, a wonderfully graphic and interesting book.

constitution, which has been created, and is still sustained, by the labours of a number of men as patriotic as himself, and with much more experience of human affairs. Little as he suspects it too, the individual whom he gibbets as "Mr. Straight" began his public career, as every Victorian knows, as a nominee of the anti-democratic party. The superfine local grandees of Brighton, a fashionable seaside suburb of Melbourne, rejected the present Chief-Justice of Victoria, and returned to Parliament in his stead the subject of Mr. Finch-Hatton's gibes.

It is, in fact, only another instance that the antipopular party in Victoria has often been the antipatriotic one. Let us by all means frankly admit that colonial democracy, like every other human movement or institution, is full of imperfection. But let us at the same time make some approach to fair-dealing and justice. What is called "society" has perhaps grown to some extent alienated from politics in these young democracies. But whose fault is this? To my mind it is largely, though I do not say altogether, the fault of that small section of wealthy colonists, who arrogate superiority over their neighbours, purely on account of their bank balance. In no place is real superiority more readily appreciated than in the colonies, but nowhere is the counterfeit article more quickly detected and exposed. It was in Victoria that the biting phrase "the *wealthy* lower orders" was first uttered. Go where you will, politics is a rough-and-tumble, and there are many refined persons in England who would be quite out of place in the House of Commons. I guarantee that if Mr. Finch-Hatton, who has a politician's instincts and aspirations, were to make his home in Victoria, he would find his way very readily into the Legislative Assembly, and would soon regard the public movements of the colony in a very different light from that of the small and publicly impotent section of colonial society with which, like most aristocratic visitors, he appears, almost exclusively, to have come in contact, and from whom he has formed his ideas, if not of Queensland, at least of Victorian politics.

In a less recent diatribe against Victorian democracy, I find it stated that "one result of it is to exclude any man of inconveniently refined temperament, of a too fastidious intellect, and an oppressively severe independence of opinion, from any part in the representation of the colony." A very little

AUSTRALIAN DEMOCRACY

time after this was written, Mr. Charles Henry Pearson, sometime Fellow of Oriel, and author of the *History of England in the Middle Ages*, was elected for such essentially working-class constituencies as Castlemaine and the East Bourke Boroughs, by the votes of diggers and quarry-men. He is now the Minister of Education in Victoria.

Of all Englishmen who have ever recorded their impressions of the Australian colonies, no one, in my judgment, has done so with so much political discrimination as Sir Charles Dilke. Though originally written twenty years ago, the two chapters in *Greater Britain* entitled "Colonial Democracy," and "Protection," may be read to this day as models of fairness and good-sense. Very different is the estimate that Sir Charles formed of the public men of the colonies from that of Mr. Finch-Hatton. For that gentleman's special behoof, as I know at heart he is really well disposed towards Australia, I will quote a brief passage from the admirable chapter on "Colonial Democracy":—

"That men of ability and character are proscribed has been one of the charges brought against colonial democracy. For my part, I found gathered in Melbourne, at the University, at the Observatory, at the Botanical Gardens, and at the Government Offices, men of the highest scientific attainments, drawn from all parts of the world, and tempted to Australia by large salaries voted by the democracy. The statesmen of all the colonies are well worthy of the posts they hold. Mr. Macalister in Queensland, and Mr. (Sir James) Martin at Sydney, are excellent debaters. Mr. (Sir Henry) Parkes, whose biography will be the typical history of a successful colonist. . . . The business powers of the present Colonial Treasurer of New South Wales are remarkable; and Mr. Higinbotham, the present Attorney-General of Victoria, possesses a fund of experience and a power of foresight which it would be hard to equal at home."

The entire chapter, as I have indicated, is specially deserving the attention of that class of itinerant Englishmen who, by reason of their own social status, are too apt to be duped by the superfine and dissatisfied type of colonist, whom even Sir Charles Dilke had to encounter in the person of the "Government clerk," who assured him that "the three last Ministers at the head of his department had been 'so low in the social scale that my wife could not visit theirs.'" Unlike Mr. Finch-Hatton, however, Sir Charles Dilke preferred to form his own estimate of Australian public men.

If the impartial critic turns to the measures passed into law, or agitated for, by the democratic party, he will also find that the *aim*, even if the means be sometimes indefensible, has in every case been to make the colonies a permanent abiding-place for a happy, prosperous, and contented community. This was undeniably the intention of the popular struggle against the squatters for possession of the Crown Lands. The pioneer squatters were no doubt a very vigorous and picturesque body, but it is only a rightful social evolution that their place has been largely taken in the more favoured and settled parts of the continent by a much more numerous and equally worthy generation of farmers. It has often been pointed out that some of the legislative enactments, known as popular Land Acts, have been the means of handing over vast tracts of country in fee-simple to the identical "Squatter" class who were previously content to be Crown tenants. To some extent this is true, but it has only been effected by the squatters resorting to "dummying" and other dubious practices; and if this class have profited in pocket by these means, to them also should attach the dishonour of subverting the laws of the Commonwealth. But in innumerable cases the result has been what the reformers wished— the settlement of the people on the land.

Take again the question of National Education. Here we see, throughout the entire group of colonies, the democratic or popular party determined, whatever the cost might be, that every child born in the territory should receive, free of cost to the parents, a sound elementary education. Nothing seems to have struck the young Princes, or rather their mentor, the Rev. John Dalton, so much as the lavish expenditure on public education in Australia.

"It really does come upon one with a shock of surprise to find how very small in England the total expenditure on Education is, after all. For England and Wales the whole cost of elementary education is only six and a half millions, and whereas in the United Kingdom the cost of education (science and art and all included) is 6s. a head, in many of our colonies it is 14s., and in some of the United States it is 19s.; in New South Wales it is 15s. per head of the population."—(*The Cruise of the Bacchante*, vol. i. p. 570.) These figures are near enough for all practical purposes of comparison, and they certainly show democracy in a very favourable light. If, instead of this enormous expenditure on the education of the young, we saw these colonies, which are largely the outcome of a heterogeneous lower middle-class and working-class emigration, growing more and more careless as to the training of the coming generation, then we might give ear to the lamentations of the aristocratic Jeremiahs of our time. It may be that a good deal of this money is wasted, and that much of the education thus freely given by the State only tends to increase the terrible competition, in what I may term the "quill-driving" callings of modern civic life. But this is an evil that will work its own cure. In one of the best of General Gordon's recently published letters, he has a very pertinent remark about the necessity of imparting a knowledge of handicrafts at school, particularly to gentlemen's sons. It is very evident that those who are wise in the next generation will see that their children are taught a mechanical trade, in addition to what will then be the universal acquirement of the three R's—for it may be that a handicraft will be almost as essential to every citizen in the future, as the capacity of common speech, or the power of locomotion.

After the manful manner in which Sir Charles Dilke, a professed Free-trader, has dealt with the subject of Protection, no American or Australian need feel ashamed of what is regarded as so heterodox and illiberal a fiscal creed in Great Britain. Indubitably the Victorian public men, from Mr. Richard Heales to Sir Graham Berry, the present Agent-General in London who consummated the policy of Protection in the colony, were among the foremost leaders of the local democracy. Yet I can remember when almost every person removed from the class of artisans and labourers was in favour of Free-trade. To be a "Free-trader" was indeed a mark of social superiority, and a test of one's knowledge and education. And the Protectionists, overwhelmed with local scorn, and isolated sentences from Adam Smith, were left to preach their doctrines in the highways and marketplaces of Melbourne. But the logic of events after all fought on their side. When alluvial mining ceased to remunerate its eager votaries there was the spectacle of a large able-bodied, vigorous population, who, in the language of the pitiful London beggars, had "got no work to do." But they were not of the type who would drag their weary limbs along city thoroughfares, and dole out their miseries in discordant imitation of the Neapolitan *lazzerone*, who have at least the artistic sense to import an organ and a monkey into the business. This line of life would not have suited the Ballarat miner. It was clearly necessary that *industries* of some kind should forthwith be established and fostered in the land. When in Collingwood, the working man's suburb of Melbourne, now in itself a corporate city of twenty-five or thirty thousand inhabitants, it was announced that "free soup-kitchens" had been started for the poor, a mixed feeling of panic and indignation took possession of the people. Had they wandered all those thousands of miles away from the old mother-land, and in the interval worked with the vigour of giants, only to find themselves at last *paupers*? Right or wrong, and whether it squared with Adam Smith and the economists or not, the manhood of the colony then and there decided that no manufactured articles which could possibly be made in the colony should come into the port of Melbourne, untaxed. "What shall we do with our boys?" exclaimed a despairing Protectionist to Mr. (afterwards Sir John) O'Shanassy, always a consistent Free-trader—"Marry them to our girls!" said he with the proverbial readiness of an Irishman. But such an answer, though it might provoke a smile even on earnest faces, was of course no solution of the difficulty in which the colony found herself through the failure of the alluvial diggings. After the manner of colonists the entire fiscal policy of Victoria was changed with amazing rapidity. A Cabinet composed mainly of avowed Free-traders introduced the first Protectionist tariff, and since then the tendency has been to increase rather than diminish the duties.[1] No Protectionist can possibly put the case fairer than does Sir Charles Dilke in the chapter of his admirable work to which I have already alluded :—

"The question of Protection," he says, "is bound up with the wider one of whether we are to love our fellow-subjects, our race, or the world at large ; whether we are to pursue our country's good at the expense of other nations ?" The working men of Collingwood, as soon as they beheld the parochial soup-kitchen, at once decided in favour of the local and patriotic, rather than the cosmopolitan theory

---

[1] Victoria, having only a limited area, is now suffering from "over-production" and wants outside markets ; hence, say her critics, her anxiety to "federate" with the other colonies.

AUSTRALIAN DEMOCRACY

But as our greatest poet, as well as greatest philosopher, tells us—

> "There's a divinity that shapes our ends,
> Rough-hew them how we will."

So even out of this petty network of hostile local tariffs, under which each colony shows such an irritating disposition to levy duties on its neighbour's productions, and where so many combine to shut out the teeming industries of the mother country, there may yet be evolved a homogeneous system of British and colonial free-trade. This cannot be done thoughtlessly without producing disastrous results, as I have elsewhere indicated with regard to Victoria; nor would the Protectionist colonies ever enter into any Zollverein with Great Britain, unless with an understanding as to the exclusion of foreign products and industries in a manner apparently subversive of Cobden's most cherished theories. As a matter of mere abstract economic science, nobody can dispute the truth of free-trade. Not only, as Sir Charles Dilke points out, is it the cosmopolitan theory; but if the British Empire is an empire in anything but name, there should certainly be the freest interchange of commodities within its borders throughout the whole of its world-wide territory. Were it possible, then, to bring the great and growing sections of our empire to trade without restriction among themselves, though with a system of " Protection" or "reciprocity," as the case may be, *against*, or *in favour of*, foreign nations, surely a great advance would have been made even from Adam Smith's standpoint on the present state of things, when this country remains alone, preaching and practising a doctrine which even her children ignore or deride.

On this point a very suggestive conversation took place between one of the most representative of the young statesmen of Australia who attended the Colonial Conference in Downing Street, and a veteran English Free-trader of world-wide fame.

"Why," said the Englishman, "do you colonists come all the way to London to settle the matter of your own defences?"

"Because," said the Australian, "we recognise that we are a portion of the British Empire, and the question of common defence is an Imperial question. We meet in London as the centre, because we regard this as the mother country, and ourselves as the offspring."

"That is the reason, I suppose," interjected the

old Free-trader, "why you exclude English products—a strange way for the offspring to behave to the mother country."

"You overlook," said the colonist, "that under the present British system of one-sided free-trade, we, the offspring, are simply placed on the same footing as the most hostile of foreign states. It is you who do not show towards us those feelings of partiality which, in individuals, are considered worthy of all praise as being parental, and according to the instincts of nature."

It must already have struck the English reader that, with all the talk about Australian democracy, the number of public men in the colonies with "handles" to their names is somewhat portentous. Yet any colonist who has arrived at middle age can remember the creation of the entire batch of K. C. M. G.'s, and other colonial knights, who, it must be confessed, have taken very kindly to the distinctive appellation of "Sir." It is true that at first when the order of St. Michael and St. George, originally intended, according to Sir George Grey, for "Maltese and Italians," was relegated to "distinguished colonists," there was a feeling against it, as though, like some kinds of merchandise, it was of an inferior quality and brand, "designed for colonial exportation." I remember hearing Mr. Higinbotham, then in the full tide of his amazing popularity, refer to the two orders of knighthood reserved for colonists in terms of intense bitterness. Like Dr. Johnson when questioned by Boswell as to his views on Voltaire and Rousseau, Mr. Higinbotham declared of these knighthoods that it was "impossible to discriminate their relative baseness." He had heard that Mr. Francis had been offered a title, but he trusted that his old political ally, " the rough virtues of whose very fine and manly character" he declared he warmly admired, would never descend to the degradation of accepting such an invidious distinction. The result of this speech was that Mr. Francis never did accept a title; and Mr. Higinbotham himself has of course consistently declined it. But with these two exceptions—to which must now be added that of Mr. Higinbotham's most promising disciple, Mr. Alfred Deakin, the youthful Chief Secretary of Victoria— I can recall no other public man in Australasia who has not cheerfully accepted a K. C. M. G.-ship, though several have declined the mere C. M. G. as being beneath their own opinion of their deserts. On the whole, then, this recent system of recognising the merits of distinguished colonists would seem to be generally acceptable even to the most democratic leaders of Australian public opinion.

But while on this subject I would like to allude to a matter originally brought before the colonial public, by Mr. (now Sir) Robert Stout. That eminent New Zealand democrat set forth his opinions in an article called "Titles for Colonists," which was originally published in the *Melbourne Review* of July 1881. It is generally thought by that numerous class of persons who seem to acquire what they are pleased to regard as information from the comic journals, and who, for instance, dispose of the Darwinian theory by expatiating on the absurdity of the notion that man could have been descended from the monkey, that Sir Robert Stout, after writing such an article, subsequently stultified himself when he accepted a knighthood. Of course such persons either have never read or have not understood Sir Robert Stout's Essay on "Titles for Colonists." The first point insisted upon in that very excellent article arose out of the conflict of opinion between Sir George Grey and Lord Carnarvon, then Secretary of State for the colonies, who had notified to the Governor of New Zealand that the Queen was graciously pleased to approve of the title of "Honourable" being borne for life by two retired judges *within the colony*. This anomalous distinction, be it further observed, was conferred on the two ex-judges without consulting either the New Zealand Parliament, or even the Premier Sir George Grey, who very properly asked Lord Carnarvon the following pertinent question—" Can the Crown, after the grant of such a constitution to this country, create and establish in New Zealand, without the consent of the General Assembly, an order of rank and dignity which does not exist in Great Britain, which is to be confined within the limit of the islands of New Zealand, and the probable direct tendency of which (in the belief of many of the people of the colony) may be to bring about ultimately a separation of New Zealand from the Empire, because it establishes here a *quasi*-aristocracy which will have no recognised rank or position in any part of the Empire outside this dependency of the Crown ? "

Nothing could be more clearly expressed than this ; and it will be observed that Sir George Grey's objection was not to the conferring of a title itself on the colonists, but that the particular title in question was a merely local and an invidious one.

Subsequent to this, Sir George Grey had a fresh

conflict with Sir Michael Hicks-Beach, on a grant of knighthood having been made to two prominent members of the Opposition in the New Zealand House of Representatives without the consent of the Governor's responsible advisers, the local Cabinet. Here, it will be seen, the ground of Sir George Grey's opposition was entirely different from that which he raised in the case of the retired judges. Let me quote it fully in his own words:—

"To illustrate the remarks I have to make, I take the case of Sir W. Fox. The honour conferred on him—knighthood—is one known to the Constitution. It emanated from the proper source—the Crown, the fountain of honour. But the recognised rule is that such honours are only conferred by the Crown upon proper responsible advice. The Crown would not in England confer a peerage upon two leading members of the Opposition without consulting its actual responsible advisers before it adopted such a course."

It will thus be seen that Sir George Grey boldly raised a very broad and important issue, and one which, I think, will have to be met in a fair and impartial spirit by some not remote British Cabinet. It was on this point that Sir Robert Stout took the side of Sir George Grey in his contention against Sir Michael Hicks-Beach, as to the impropriety of the practice of conferring titles on colonists without the consent or recommendation of the local ministry. In justice to Sir Robert Stout, who has been most widely misrepresented even in the colonies, I will, at the risk of dwelling at undue length on the subject, quote his summary of the entire argument:

"It was the consideration of the right of creating a new order for the colonies, not recognised throughout the Empire, that led the Grey Government to comment on the despatches of August 29, 1877. If the Empire is one, how can it be said that the Crown has the right to limit the use of a title to one portion of the Empire? It is on the theory of unity that the Sovereign has the right of interference with the colonies; and one of the reasons given for the grant of titles to colonists is that such tends to mould the Empire into one. But if a title is only to be known in one colony, does not that at once create a separation and division which must, in its influence, do more harm than good? Besides, this is creating something unknown to the land, and in a colony where there is representative government—creating it without the sanction or concurrence of either the Colonial Parliament or the Colonial Ministry. On what ground can such a proceeding be defended?

"Coming now to the second question, viz., On whose advice should titles be granted? It may be remarked that if the titles are to be only colonial titles, not to be used beyond the colony, it should be the function of the Colonial Ministry to advise as to their bestowal. The Colonial Ministers are responsible to the Colonial Parliament, and to colonial public opinion for the advice they tender. If it was to be an Imperial distinction, no doubt much, at any rate, could be said for the Imperial Ministry being responsible for the honours conferred—though even in that case it is submitted the Colonial Executive should be consulted. For how can the Imperial Ministry know what colonists should be rewarded? What does the English Parliament know, and what can it know, of the colonists to whom distinctions are granted? If a Colonial Ministry on such a question tendered advice that was not backed by public opinion, their constituents have a ready means of calling them to account. Why, then, should a Colonial Ministry be placed in a position different from that of an English Ministry?"

In bringing to a close these somewhat casual observations on the democracy of the colonies, I may perhaps be permitted to reiterate my sense of the many imperfections and errors which must inevitably disfigure the career of King Demos as of every other earthly sovereign. Under universal suffrage, unprincipled and selfish men will clamber into the chambers of legislature just as, under a very different system, they have found their way into the palaces of kingly and priestly potentates. To such a pitch has the system reached of harassing the Executive, by the abuse of Parliamentary forms, that Mr. Alfred Deakin, whom Lord Knutsford will remember at the Colonial Conference, on his return to Victoria proclaimed that a remedy must be found, even if some points of the American Constitution are adopted in lieu of the English methods that colonists have hitherto followed. Let us be sure of one thing, that when such a change is deemed essential for the salvation of the State, it will be made in the twinkling of an eye. Nor will any one venture to propose that the Irreconcilables should be bought off by giving them a separate province to themselves to misgovern without let or hindrance. This is, after all, the strong side of what I must call a " Conservative democracy "—like that of Victoria. In such a community almost every man is actively on the side of law and order. When Mr. James Service returned to Melbourne from the Colonial Conference, he was naturally asked what he thought of the Trafalgar Square riots. Although an active politician, desirous of remaining in favour with the colonial working classes, the Victorian ex-Premier at once launched out into hearty laudations of the conduct of Sir Charles Warren and the police. He had seen the whole affair, he said, from his window in Morley's Hotel, and he thought it was a more or less organised attempt on the part of the loafers and the unemployed to create a disturbance. "The conduct of the police," he added, "was most admirable and most forbearing." Now these are the words, it must be remembered, of a colonial public man, whose position depends mainly on the vote of the working classes. And we see he speaks out as plainly as only John Bright can speak in this country, on such a question as the murder of poor Sergeant Brett by the Manchester Fenians. The reason of the difference is that the colonial statesman is more in " touch " with the great mass of his fellow-countrymen, and therefore can afford to denounce in very plain terms any symptoms of national crime or public hysteria, which crafty or misguided men may be fostering to the peril of the community.

Perhaps I may here be permitted to allude to certain conversations I had on public matters with Mr. Service, whom I have elsewhere described as "a typical Australian statesman." As he was then attending the Colonial Conference in Downing Street, our conversation very naturally took a turn in the direction of the enormous outlay on modern armaments. I maintained, I remember, that the working classes could not be expected to support this heavy taxation very cheerfully; and that therefore a democracy might be at a severe disadvantage in the terrible "struggle for existence" against a despotically governed state. I was struck with Mr. Service's reply. He said: "For my part, if I were convinced of the necessity of an enormously increased outlay for defensive purposes, I should never be afraid to apply to the working classes for it. Only I should make it clear that every penny I asked for would, as far as possible, be expended for that purpose, and not be frittered away in ornamental salaries."

On another occasion, in an equally pessimistic mood, I chose to quote, or perhaps rather to distort, Lord Wolseley, to the effect that the British must inevitably fall behind the French and Germans unless they would willingly submit to the "discipline of the conscription." Mr. Service very properly thought that no people would "willingly" submit to the conscription. But he gave me to understand that, in his opinion, if a foreign coast could be seen from Wilson's Promontory as plainly as the French coast from Dover, and if the Victorians knew that on those foreign shores there were a million armed men, the conscription would be cheerfully undergone without a day's delay. And not only with Mr. Service, but perhaps even stronger with Sir Graham Berry and other popular leaders of Australia, I have noticed the same disposition to trust in the general good sense of the people, or, in cases of emergency, where the masses seem misdirected, to speak out without equivocation what must be at the time the most unpalatable truths. This is, I know, not according to the preconceived ideas of many persons, and therefore in dealing with the subject I purposely record my own personal experiences.

It is the same if you turn to the most democratic newspapers in Australia, wherever they are serious and intended to instruct as well as amuse their myriad readers. In the *Leader*, which, with the *Age*, forms what has been called the "working man's Bible" in Victoria, one lights constantly on such pithy paragraphs as this:—

"Mr. O'Brien, who whines over his breeches, is, according to the *Pall Mall Gazette*, of 'the kinglier breed,' a hero of the old heroic strain."

Only this, and nothing more; and in these brief words the whole sickening cant about "the patriot's martyrdom," which was for a time a main staple in certain English journals, aiming to be democratic, is thus disposed of in a colonial paper that is not only democratic itself, but exists in a purely democratic atmosphere. It is all the difference between the player-king and the genuine potentate.

Arising out of this, too, it seems to me that the average intelligent Australian forms a far fairer estimate of our American kinsmen than is prevalent in England. It is a suggestive fact, and one which I think makes for the inevitable alliance of the English-speaking peoples who now claim so magnificent a portion of this world's estate, that the heroes of American history have already taken their place among the traditional heroes of the English-speaking world. Unconsciously we have all come to recognise that George Washington and Benjamin Franklin were as great leaders of what Dr. Freeman calls the "English folk movement," as any in the mere insular story from Alfred the Great, to Arthur, Duke of Wellington. It is only by so reading the history of our race that we can ever comprehend the great part we have played, and are still destined to play, in the history of the world. It is in this spirit that a thoughtful Australian, though his heart goes forth in the first place to the *mother* country—to the "isle of blowing woodland, isle of silvery parapets," yet has a profound and undying interest in the story that is in some respects more akin to his own, the great story of the colonisation and civilisation of America, by men and women who also

"Speak the language Shakespeare spoke,
The faith and morals hold that Milton held."

If asked suddenly who he regards as *our* greatest man in modern times, the reflective Australian would be not unlikely to answer "Abraham Lincoln," and in so answering would pay a profounder tribute to the greatness of our race than if he had named any one of the contemporary worthies of Great Britain. This state of feeling I hold to be an outcome, in great measure, of Australian democracy. I remember an American saying, with much truth, that to judge from the English papers there were only two people on the great American continent worth writing about, O'Donovan Rossa and Mrs. Langtry—" the one," he said, " a beautiful, and the other a very ugly, fleeting bubble on the great sea of American public life; and neither of them Americans." I have elsewhere, however, said enough on this point, as affecting the colonies.

In conclusion, I only ask the English reader to accept the situation as he finds it, and make the best of it. The democracies of Australia are far from perfect, but they cannot be sneered out of existence; and if we believe in the inherent vigour, veracity, and manliness of our race, they may yet be made important factors in our Empire, and sources of strength rather than of weakness to the mother-land. That they contain many disturbing elements, and that they may on occasion exhibit a low standard of national life mainly by reason of those elements, it will be the purpose of the two succeeding chapters in some measure to illustrate.

CHAPTER V.

AUSTRALIA AND IRISH HOME RULE.

It may be remembered that at a political banquet in London on St. Patrick's Day, Mr. Parnell, with characteristic boldness, declared that Australia, as well as America, had become "solid" in favour of Irish Home Rule. After this it was hardly to be wondered at that two of his Parliamentary followers who had never seen Australia were deputed to respond on behalf of my unhappy section of the British Empire. This banquet, which, but for the unwonted intrusion of Australia into its post-prandial oratory, was in no wise remarkable, took place only a few months ago, but already a wonderful transformation in Mr. Parnell's political creed seems to have been effected. When, at the Café Royal, he asserted that we Australians were "solid on his side," I, in common with the rest of my fellow-colonists, understood him to mean that we favoured Mr. Gladstone's Home Rule Bill. But since then Mr. Parnell, to judge by his published correspondence with a South African politician, has become—(O shade of William Edward Forster!)—an Imperial Federationist. It is idle, if not mischievous, to inquire too closely into the motives of public men, but certainly this entire *volte-face* on the part of a man so tenaciously immovable as Mr. Parnell has hitherto shown himself to be, is in itself a more remarkable circumstance than the conversion of Mr. Gladstone to Irish Home Rule, or to any other political or religious creed under the face of the sun.

With regard to Australia and Irish Home Rule let me then say that the great bulk of the Australian colonists saw, from the very first introduction of Mr. Gladstone's bill, that its fatal defect was that it set up what Mr. Parnell now terms a "dualism." On this account it seemed to us, from an Imperial point of view, the most retrograde and most destructive of measures. But we further judged from Mr. Parnell's actions and speeches that what to us was a detestable blot, was to him an unblemished beauty. In other words, we were of opinion that his ultimate aim, which he was too cynical even to conceal, was the dismemberment of the Empire. Certainly—and Mr. Parnell would now appear to agree with us rather than with his most distinguished follower—no readier means for such dismemberment could have been devised than what we may now fairly enough consider the defunct Home Rule Bill of Mr. Gladstone. Mr. Parnell tells us that he is now opposed to the "dualism" of Mr. Gladstone's abortive measure. At the same time, I do not think that many wealthy Australians will be prepared to follow the example of Mr. Rhodes, of South Africa, in contributing handsomely to the funds of the Irish Parliamentary party, under the conviction that it may become an agency for the "closer union of the Empire." When Mr. Parnell declared that we Australians were "solid on his side," he meant on the side of what he now discards as "dualism." Moreover, it has always been in this light that his revolutionary countrymen, both in Ireland and America, have regarded what was to them at best merely a tentative and half-way measure. Now, as it were by the magician's wand, all is to be changed. Ireland is to have her local or national Parliament, but there are to be Irish representatives in some freshly-constructed Parliamentary body at Westminster. Let me give the rest of the picture in Mr. Parnell's reported words :—

"After Ireland has had some experience of Home Rule, the Scotch people will probably require to have their Parliament at Holyrood, but they will certainly insist upon their continued representation at Westminster. This may have, as its ultimate development, the establishment of a Federal Parliament, in which England, Scotland, Ireland, Wales, and the Colonies will be represented. It would seem likely, therefore, that the House of Commons will become a purely English assembly, while the Imperial Parliament will be a new body that will take the place of the House of Lords, and will become possessed of representatives from all the self-governing countries and colonies which make up the British Empire." "This, of course," adds Mr. Parnell, with characteristic caution, "is a long way off."

I do not propose to discuss the Irish leader's shadowy scheme of Imperial Federation. But as I have asserted that he was absurdly wrong in claiming that the Australian colonists are in favour of Mr. Gladstone's Home Rule Bill, so I venture to think it may be of benefit, both to him and to the ordinary British politician, to realise what the prevailing colonial sentiment is on the so-called Irish Question. Roughly speaking, it may be declared that by origin the Australians are three-fourths British and one-fourth Irish. Among that fourth, however strong may be the sympathy with the Constitutional agitation in favour of Irish Home Rule, it is absolutely true that no trace exists of a section analogous to the Irish-American dynamite party. Australia has never nurtured a bloodthirsty braggart such as O'Donovan Rossa, or a journalistic firebrand like Patrick Ford, nor from her shores have ever emerged any of those subsidised assassins and murderers who have from time to time crossed the Atlantic on their barbaric crusade. Generally speaking, the Irish element in Australia, though many of its members may support the Land League and secretly sympathise with boycotting—13,000 miles away—is avowedly faithful to the British Crown and connection. In a sketch, by a Roman Catholic writer, of the late Sir John O'Shanassy (*Melbourne Review*, July 1883), admittedly the greatest of Irish-Australian politicians, appears the following suggestive statement :—

" While he (O'Shanassy) was ill, he was waited

upon with a view of inducing him to take the chair for the Brothers Redmond. He refused to have anything to do with them. He had not invited them. He would not receive them. He was not satisfied as to where the League money went to. He was grieved to hear the clergy were likely to countenance them, and believed that evil would result therefrom."

Mr. Parnell can easily find out whether this was the treatment actually accorded to his two emissaries in Melbourne. For my part, I can assure him that he would have met with no greater courtesy from Sir John O'Shanassy, even had he waited upon him personally. I admit that the sudden conversion of Mr. Gladstone, to what was hitherto simply termed " Parnellism," was not without its demoralising effect on the Australian public mind. Colonial Irishmen, who had previously been restrained, began to give vent to their racial antagonisms, and, of course, there was the usual percentage of flabby-minded and hysterical persons who were quite prepared to accept the new creed of Mr. Gladstone in lieu of what, for a better term, I must call their own convictions. But these latter were inconsiderable both in numbers and in influence. It is undeniably true that the great bulk of the Australian colonists are now, as they were from the first, steadily opposed to any scheme of Irish Home Rule that has yet been formulated.

A few years ago a very remarkable discussion was originated in the pages of an Australian magazine by a Victorian gentleman, Mr. A. M. Topp, whose essay (*Melbourne Review*, January 1881), entitled "English Institutions and the Irish Race," excited very general interest throughout the colonies. If Mr. Gladstone and Sir William Harcourt will be good enough to endeavour to recall the scenes in the House of Commons that led to the expulsion of Mr. Parnell and thirty-six of his followers, they may perhaps understand why we colonists, about that time, were so eagerly discussing the Irish Question.

It was doubtless the earlier achievements of the Irish Parliamentary Party, emphasised by boycotting in Ireland and dynamite from America, that led Mr. Topp, who is no party politician, but a thoughtful historical student, first to turn his acute mind to this subject. The Irish Question is, according to Mr. Topp, primarily one of race. He sees in the dynamite, the boycotting, the Land League, and the Irish obstruction in the

House of Commons (and would continue to see in the "plan of campaign"), only varying phases of the same Celtic revolt against Teutonic institutions. Having resolved the Anglo-Irish problem into one of race, Mr. Topp is at considerable pains to distinguish between the Irish Celt, or the aboriginal Irishman, and the Anglo-Irishman, who, though a native of Ireland, is of English or Scotch extraction. Like Mr. Froude, he will not for a moment admit that the Duke of Wellington and Daniel O'Connell, or Lord Wolseley and Mr. T. P. O'Connor, though all natives of Ireland, are racially of the same stock. Mr. Topp has a very handy crook wherewith to divide the sheep from the goats, the real aboriginal Irish, whom he alleges to be very generally in a state of open or suppressed revolt against English institutions, and the acclimatised Anglo-Irish, who, though they may have furnished a certain number of leaders of the revolutionary party, are, in the main, English in race, religion, and in feeling. According to him, the test is one of creed; the Irish Celt is a Roman Catholic, the Anglo-Irishman a Protestant. On this point I think Mr. Topp's words require some explanation. I should warn the English reader that it would be very rash to bring any hasty charge of religious bigotry against this able Australian writer. Mr. Topp is, from conviction, based on historical research, a decided anti-Romanist, but in his mind there is no silly prejudice against the greatest and most remarkable of all ecclesiastical organisations. "Every student of history," he observes, "will readily admit that the Church of Rome has conferred great benefits on mankind in times past, and was once, perhaps, the greatest civilising agent in Europe." He pays a passing tribute, which is not undeserved, to the old Roman Catholic families in England; for, despite isolated acts of treason which brought a swift punishment in the troubled times of the Tudors and of James I., the small remnant of the English gentry who tenaciously clung to Rome as their spiritual guide have often shown a brave fidelity to their Sovereign and their race.[1] But Mr. Topp's excuse for not dwelling on this point is that the handful of Roman Catholic gentry count for very little one way or the other in the solution of the Irish Question; and in proof of this he could point to the recent attitude of Cardinal Manning, who, immediately before the Papal Rescript, made no secret of his sympathy

[1] See Appendix D, "Religion and Irish Home Rule."

with the Home Rule views and methods of the Archbishop of Dublin. Despite the neo-Catholic fashions of the hour, Mr. Topp stoutly maintains that the essential inferiority of the Celt to the Teuton is historically shown by the fact that the English and the Germans "broke with" Rome three centuries ago, while the French and the Irish did not. For my part, I hold that racial distinctions are much deeper than religious differences. Mr. Gee and some of the Welsh Protestant anti-tithe agitators would soon assimilate their methods to those of Mr. Davitt and the Irish Land League. Blood is thicker than water, even when the water is from the font. Still I freely admit that credal differences always intensify, and may perpetuate, racial distinctions.

This question of race is, according to other authorities besides Mr. Topp, of vital importance. Mr. Michael Davitt, who has suffered and run personal risks in this melancholy cause, made some suggestive remarks recently on the "Mission of the Celts." According to him, the Irish Celt is "in the vanguard of the glorious struggle of labour against systems, and laws which condemn the cottier of Connemara and the crofter of Scotland to live in miserable hovels, while idle and loafing aristocrats could revel upon the result of others' labours and live in sumptuous mansions." The grand mission of his race was, he explained, to lead the coming social and political revolution which is to sweep away these gross anomalies, but he fails to see that this would, were it successful, also overwhelm the long-matured system of law and social order, of culture, science, and religion, which mark this country out as the home of an ancient, progressive, and civilised nation. But let it be observed that Mr. Davitt agrees with Mr. Topp that the Irish Question is *au fond* a question of race. Mr. Topp supports this view by a reference to the inimitable description by the great historian Mommsen of the character of the Celts of Gaul, who "on the eve of their conquest by Cæsar resembled the modern Irish." This racial view of the Celts, I may add, has impressed itself on the mind of the greatest maker, as well as of the greatest writer, of history of our times.

"'The Teutonic or Germanic race,' said Bismarck,[1] with his customary point and pungency, 'is, so to speak, the masculine element which goes all over

---

[1] *Bismarck in the Franco-German War*, by Dr. Busch, vol. ii. p. 285.

Europe and fructifies it. The Celtic and Slav peoples represent the female sex. The former element extends up to the North Sea and across it to England.'

"'I venture to say,' interrupted Dr. Busch, 'even to America; to the Western States of the Union, where men of our race are the best part of the population, and influence the *morale* of the rest.'

"'Yes; they are its children, its fruits,' responded Bismarck. 'We have already seen in France what the Franks are worth; the Revolution of 1789 meant the overthrow of the German element by the Celtic; and what is the result?'"

This will probably be a new, enlarged, and most enlivening view of the "mission of the Celts" to Mr. Davitt. It is at least suggestive that the great German Chancellor, the colonial publicist, and the Irish revolutionary, are in substantial agreement on this vital point.

It will readily be believed that Mr. Topp's essay on "English Institutions and the Irish Race" created no little stir among a population one-fourth of which is of Irish origin. The *Melbourne Review* was conducted on what are known as eclectic principles, and its conductors welcomed the champions of all phases of opinion. Among the literary contributors to the *Review* were one or two well-known Roman Catholic priests, but they preserved a discreet silence. There came instead a really able reply by Mr. Joseph O'Brien, an Irish gentleman then resident at Sandhurst, Victoria, who, proud of the fact that he was of Celtic race, declared, with hardly less pride, that he had " broken with Rome." Although this was the only reply that reached the conductors of the *Melbourne Review*, it was not through an avowed agnostic like Mr. O'Brien that the Irish Celts in the colony delivered their retort. The priests, as I have said, though contributors to the periodical, chose not to reply in the usual way, but there was a considerable pother throughout the land, and even threats of personal violence were made towards the opener of this instructive controversy.

After this brief summary of an interesting symposium, I will now explain my own views—which, I believe, are the views of the majority of Australian colonists—on the subject. While feeling bound to follow such authorities as Prince Bismarck, Mr. Davitt, and Mr. Topp, who, it would seem, all hold that race is the *crux* of the problem, I do not think, in dealing with such a question as

Irish Home Rule, that the pessimistic attitude of such writers as Mr. Froude is a wise one. Mr. Topp, too, I fear, is touched by the same spirit of despair, for he even laments, if I understand him rightly, the granting of "Catholic emancipation," regarding that act apparently as putting the most effective weapon—viz., a vote—into the hands of a people racially hostile to English law. But, after all, practical politics are only a choice of evils, and the Irish Roman Catholics must have been enfranchised or reconquered. Still, I admit that it does not lighten the task to have thus "armed" a race whom we must assimilate, or who may otherwise weaken, if not destroy, the fabric of our Empire.

Let us, however, never forget that the British Empire is based on a blending of races and nationalities originally fiercely antagonistic. Both Lord Hartington and Mr. Balfour, in addressing Scotch audiences recently, have felicitously emphasised the fact that Scotland offers the most perfect illustration of the possibility of welding the Celt and the Teuton into a common nationality; and, furthermore, of subsequently making that blended nationality the most loyal, intelligent, and enterprising portion of a world-wide Empire. The present Unionists are those men who believe that what has been accomplished in Scotland can be accomplished in the wider area of Great Britain and Ireland, and that the Irish may yet become as thoroughly fused with the British as the Highlanders have become with the Lowlanders of Scotland. It is at least a noble ideal, and one well worth working and even fighting for. The undue oratorical development of our Parliamentary system is an obstacle in the way; for all this talk, even when clever, is a mere frittering of human energies. It is also as well for us to bear steadily in mind that if the Celtic races have grave national defects of character, so too have the Teutons. I cannot do better than quote Prince Bismarck's inimitable criticism on the German national character, which is quite equal to his analysis of the French, and which is, word for word, as applicable to the English and the Lowland Scotch as his estimate of the French is to the Irish.

The great Chancellor begins[1] by showing what a dominant part the Germans have played *outside* their own country in establishing nations and dynasties:—

[1] *Bismarck in the Franco-German War*, by Dr. Busch, vol. ii. p. 285.

"In Spain, too, the Gothic blood long preponderated; and the same in Italy, where the Germans had also taken the lead in the northern provinces; when that died away, farewell to order. It was much the same in Russia where the German Waräger, the Ruriks, first gathered. If the national party were to overcome the Germans who have settled there, or those who cross over from the Baltic provinces, the people would not remain capable of an orderly constitution."

But he goes on to show that *within* their own territories the "pure-blooded Germans" had a fatal tendency to split up into what are called "parties" in politics and "sects" in religion.

"In our South and West, for example, when they were left to themselves, there was nothing but Knights of the Empire, Towns of the Empire, and Villages of the Empire; each for itself, so that the whole thing went to pieces. The Germans are all right when they are united by compulsion or by anger, then they are excellent, irresistible, invincible,—*otherwise, every man 'gangs his ain gait.'*"

It is suggestive that he should thus emphasise his meaning by a Lowland Scotch proverb!

On another occasion he pithily contrasts this

racial distinction in a manner which we Anglo-Saxons would do well to ponder :—

"The French are a mass easily brought under the influence of one leader, and are then very powerful. With us every one has his own opinion; and with Germans it is a great step gained when any considerable number of them hold the same opinion—if they all did so, they would be omnipotent."

Have we not here in a sentence the whole history of the relations between England and Ireland? Certainly, one would not like to hear of Englishmen blindly following a leader, as the Irish have followed Mr. Parnell. Still less of their abjectly submitting to the boycotting commands of some village tyrant with his Plan of Campaign. But in the face of recent developments of national character in Ireland, we, with our party divisions and academic differences, have not presented at all an ennobling national spectacle. Perhaps this is what Mr. Balfour means when he talks of the Irish possessing characteristics which the English lack, and which are essential to our Imperial greatness and unity. Without doubt, if the instinct of "sticking together," which the Irish have exhibited only too often in criminal causes and for destructive ends, could be turned to account for truly Imperial aims, and for our general well-being as a people, we should well-nigh be, as Bismarck says, "omnipotent."

What, after all, in the fewest words, is the Irish problem of practical politics? Writers like Mr. Froude and Mr. Topp seem to be of opinion that we have been travelling on the wrong road, and must retrace our steps. This is, unless as the result of revolution, impossible, for "there is no coming back on the impetuous stream of Life, and we must all set our pocket-watches by the clock of Fate." It is from this point of view I hold that the Liberal-Unionists have already won a distinct place in our Parliamentary annals, and deserve the plaudits of every loyal man in the Empire. They have remained true to Liberalism, and at the same time loyal to the great English system of law, out of which Liberalism has sprung. By their political patriotism they have preserved us from that "dualism" which Mr. Parnell now sees would be a catastrophe to the Empire. All thoughtful persons in the great self-governing colonies who are assisting to work out the English system of Parliamentary Government must await the present issue with bated breath. No one will accuse Mr. Froude of want of patriotism, but it would appear that he has resigned himself to a general "smash up." The Parliamentary machine, he believes, will not work while Ireland clogs the wheels. Above all, the conduct of Mr. Gladstone, and of his great following in the country and in Parliament, are, to men like Mr. Froude, portents of coming evil. But I think, perhaps, that Mr. Gladstone's opponents, as well as his disciples, overrate his lasting influence, by which I mean the effect his career will produce on the coming generations. We colonists hold—and Mr. Parnell now seems to have come to the same opinion—that Mr. Gladstone has fallen into grievous ways towards the close of his remarkable career. We have recognised from the first that his great error consists in thinking that the long struggle between what he now calls "the two nations" would end if his statutory Parliament were established in Dublin. Rightly considered, it would then only begin in real earnest. Mr. Froude and his colonial disciple, Mr. Topp, seeing all this plainly enough, overrate while they attack the personality of Mr. Gladstone, and under-estimate the vigour and the vitality of the English race. They should take heart from the instinctive conduct of that other great Liberal leader, John Bright, a man to whom all mere grandiose Imperial views are foreign—a Liberal of Liberals, but who yet, when a blow is aimed even by Mr. Gladstone at a vital part of the body politic, strikes back with giant force. Let us then recognise that to Lord Hartington and the distinguished men who have faithfully followed him, and who have remained firm in the hour of weak tergiversation and dark misgiving, we owe it that the "dualism" which Mr. Parnell now discards is not already in the way of fulfilment. Let us hold with them that by patient patriotism and the healing virtues of time, it is possible to solve the Irish Question, which must be solved by us at the extremity, as by you in the centre, of this complex Empire. What would be thought of the British in Australia if they seriously proposed to give the Irish minority a separate Parliament and distinct Executive? The future is still dark. But difficult and unpleasant as the task may be, the British people must assimilate, and, as it were, work the Irish into the ground-plan of the Empire, and not, as Mr. Gladstone would bid us do, relinquish the task in a spirit of panic-stricken despair.

CHAPTER VI.

THE IRISH IN AUSTRALIA.

THE Australians, as I have stated, are by origin three-fourths British and one-fourth Irish. Beyond a general statement to the effect that the "Irish element in Australia" is in the main "faithful to the British Crown and connection," I forbore in the preceding chapter from giving any analysis of this important section of the colonial population. But the recent publication in England of what I cannot but regard as most misleading and mischievous views on the subject impels me to offer a separate chapter on the "Irish in Australia," in which I propose to discuss their racial characteristics, especially in relation to public affairs, and to the wellbeing and continuance of the Empire.

I must at the outset call the reader's special attention to an article entitled "An Australian Example," which appeared in the *Contemporary Review* of January 1888, from the pen of Sir Charles

Gavan Duffy, formerly a leader of the "Young Ireland" party, but more recently a politician, and now a pensioner, of the Colony of Victoria; and to a recently published book, *The Irish in Australia*, by Mr. J. F. Hogan, an Irish-Australian journalist.

I must confess that the effect of this strong dose of Celtic literature on the uninstructed British mind must be truly appalling. According to both these authorities, it is the Irish who have done everything worthy of record in these so-called British colonies. If, however, one turns from the glowing, if somewhat immature, pages of Mr. Hogan to the Victorian Year-Book of Mr. H. H. Hayter, the Government Statist, one quickly re-awakens to the fact that the great bulk of the Australian people are of British descent or birth. Can it be then that the race which Lord Salisbury has proclaimed to be the "Imperial and consolidating" race in these islands has, despite its superior numbers, played but a minor *rôle* at the Antipodes?

Before attempting to deal with this interesting question, let me briefly state what I conceive to be the political intention of Sir C. Gavan Duffy's Essay, "An Australian Example." He shows that the Colony of Victoria dates its rise and progress from the day when it achieved political separation from New South Wales; when Melbourne, and not Sydney, became the seat of government. Ireland, therefore, he argues, will prosper when its laws emanate from College Green, and not from St. Stephen's. Furthermore, running throughout his pages is the assumption, that under the free and equal suffrage of democratic Victoria, the Irish Celt has quite held his own against the Anglo-Saxon colonist; and that, therefore, it would be beneficial for Ireland and not injurious to the Empire, if the government were placed in the hands of the predominant race. I cannot but think that Sir C. Gavan Duffy very much weakens the effect of his otherwise adroit literary performance by extraneous abuse of Mr. Balfour. We Victorians would at any time have hailed the brilliant Irish Chief Secretary, especially with an official "lodge" at Melbourne, as an ideal Secretary of State for the Colonies. Mr. Balfour is in fact the kind of man for whom, at least a few years ago, we used to cry out in our troubles; a statesman of initiative, possessing courage, intellect, and culture, and not a mere Downing Street drone. If Sir C. Gavan Duffy is really serious in considering the autonomy of

Victoria as an "Australian example," which Great Britain should follow in her treatment of Ireland, then I fear he is sadly deceiving himself, if not his readers. The experience he gained in the Speaker's Chair of the Legislative Assembly at Melbourne will not, I venture to think, be ever utilised by an Irish House of Commons in Dublin. With regard to the second thesis of his paper, viz., the political capacity shown by the Irish race in the colonies, a subject which is also treated *ad nauseam* by Mr. Hogan, I will now endeavour to express my own unbiassed opinions. In thus specially dealing with the "Irish in Australia," it is, however, of the very first importance to keep before one's mind the racial distinction between the Anglo-Irish and the Irish Celts. In a dim and confused way this has passed through the mind of Sir C. Gavan Duffy, even in the midst of his Home-Rule reveries. To a thoughtful reader, indeed, the most suggestive point in the whole of his Magazine article is his somewhat ambiguous confession that these Anglo-Irish colonists have been the dominant political factor in the making, if not of Australia, at least of Victoria. Whenever it serves the purpose of his argument, Sir C. Gavan Duffy is not slow to emphasise the racial distinction between what he calls the two "sections" of Irish settlers; but he more often ignores or strives to obliterate it. Mr. Hogan, on the other hand, appears quite ignorant of the fact, and his book so teems with bulls and blunders that I should seriously advise him to recast its form. As a history it is ludicrous; but there is material perhaps for an Irish-Australian prose idyll of the Paul and Virginia type, which under some such title as "Pat and Brigitta," might delight the yet unborn antipodean babe.

Sir C. Gavan Duffy is of course on an entirely different intellectual plane from Mr. Hogan, but it is lamentable to notice how readily he copies the loose and inaccurate statements to be found in *The Irish in Australia*. For instance, the late Marcus Clarke is referred to as the "one man of genius who wrote an Australian novel recognised in Europe as a masterpiece," and is on that account apparently classified as an Irishman. As a matter of fact, Clarke was born at Kensington, educated at Highgate, and never even saw Ireland; his father being an English barrister of the Middle Temple, though connected with the Anglo-Irish gentry, and his mother an actress, who was, I believe, of Jewish descent. But he wrote a very powerful novel, and so is at once claimed, first by Mr. Hogan and then by Sir C. Gavan Duffy, as a "fellow-countryman." Neither space nor patience, however, is sufficiently elastic to permit one to expose these curiously suggestive myths which have been invented, I suppose, to support Mr. Gladstone's Home-Rule proposals.

Let us, however, turn for a while to the genuine annals of Australia, when I think we shall be at once struck with the historic achievements of the Anglo-Irish colonists, whose political and intellectual ascendency reads simply like a brilliant colonial addendum to Mr. Froude's *English in Ireland*. Sir C. Gavan Duffy eulogistically refers to William Charles Wentworth, under his old and familiar *sobriquet* of "the Australian Patriot." Without altogether indorsing Dr. Johnson's familiar definition of patriotism, one can only say that the title fails to describe the supreme achievement of Wentworth, whose real place in our colonial annals is that of the political father of free Australasia. It would take a goodly volume, and one well deserving the reverent labours of a painstaking and patriotic pen, to give an adequate account of the career of this Australian "nation-builder." He gave New South Wales its constitution. He established in the colony trial by jury. He founded the Sydney University, from which has sprung every other *alma mater* at the Antipodes. That such achievements were not the results of mere good fortune, or blind chance, but were the work of a great and comprehensive political genius, will perhaps best be brought home to the minds of Englishmen, by reiterating that Wentworth's rival, both in the Senate and at the Bar of New South Wales, was Robert Lowe, and that on most occasions he proved himself quite the intellectual compeer of the future Viscount Sherbrooke.

William Charles Wentworth, who was born in New Norfolk, then a famous, or infamous, penal settlement, and educated at the University of Cambridge, was by descent Anglo-Irish; his father hailing from Ireland, but his historic name and religious creed are full evidence of his English lineage. Turning to the colony with which, like Sir C. Gavan Duffy, I am most familiar, Victoria, I too can recall the time when its intellectual princes were, with one or two exceptions, of Anglo-Irish stock. What Victorian can forget Sir William Foster Stawell, formerly Chief-Justice, now Lieutenant-Governor of the colony, a man with the singleness of purpose, and inflexibility of will, of his great countryman the Iron Duke, and who, whether as the leading politician or the highest judge, has left the impress of his character and personality like that of a die on the colony? As a judge, however, he was surpassed by the judicial temperament and legal attainments of Mr. Justice Molesworth, who for many years presided over the Equity Court, and whose decisions were often reviewed, but rarely if ever reversed, by the Privy Council. He too was born in Ireland, educated at Trinity College, Dublin, and called to the Irish bar, but was of course of an English patrician family. The late Dr. William Edward Hearn,[1] the well-known constitutional lawyer and political economist, "the greatest thinker who ever made his home in a British colony," was also of the "English garrison" of Ireland; while in Mr. George Higinbotham, who has worthily succeeded Sir William Foster Stawell in the Chief-Justiceship of Victoria, we have yet another Anglo-Irishman, who, under the widest democratic suffrage, ruled the colony, for a number of years, with almost the

[1] See Appendix G,—Obituary, Dr. Hearn.

power of a despotic sovereign, though purely by his lofty character, fine intellect, and overpowering personality.[1]

It would not be difficult to give a reason why from a poor country like Ireland, with its two antagonistic races, there should have been such a noteworthy exodus to the new El Dorado. These Anglo-Irish, high-minded, courageous, well-educated, energetic, and born with the instincts of a governing race, were exactly the kind of men to take the chief part in the founding and ruling of new colonies, such as those which had been so magically called into existence, by the gold discoveries at the Antipodes.

In the political building-up of Australia, these Anglo-Irish have indeed been like a small but powerful body of patricians, who from the first made their influence felt over the general mass of English, Scotch, and Celtic-Irish *plebs*. With regard to the purely English colonists and their descendants, who were always in a great majority, it is not denied that there was a sprinkling of men of good birth and high character who were from

[1] Sir George Grey of New Zealand is another striking illustration.

the first among the ruling caste of Australia. Still, comparatively few ambitious young Englishmen of the high type of Robert Lowe went so far afield to pick up a fortune. Among the English emigrants attracted by the gold discoveries, there were, for the most part, a number of thoroughly respectable, though in most cases unfortunate, middle-class families. With these went in shoals the οἱ πολλοί—lowly men and women,—who, however, by the very fact that they had the spirit and enterprise to cross the great waste of waters, displayed their superiority, at least in these qualities, to their equally poor and discontented but stay-at-home kinsfolk. What part, let me incidentally ask, has this great bulk of Englishry played in the making of Australia?

Were any one to take the trouble to go through the lists of Cabinet Ministers, members of Colonial Legislatures and Municipal Councils, and to examine the names in the learned professions, and those over the great houses of business, and to glance down the roll of members of the clubs and scientific and philosophic institutions, he would find that the overwhelming majority are English.

The "constitutional history of Victoria," says Sir C. Gavan Duffy truly enough, "cannot be written in a paragraph." "When it comes to be written," he proceeds, "it will be seen how large and effectual a factor were the *Irish of both sections*. It would be absurd to suggest that they were fitter than Englishmen to administer a system honourably known to the world as 'English liberty,' but they were more eager to show that they were fit, and readier to make the sacrifice which a public career involved in a gold colony, where 'be in a hurry to grow rich' was the accepted gospel."

I have fully and frankly conceded all that he can possibly demand for what he calls one "section" of the Irish, and now propose to examine the purely Celtic claims.

Sir C. Gavan Duffy quotes, with marked approval, the saying of some Scotch journalist, that they (the Celtic Irish) were "the only politicians in the colony,"—meaning the only men of the rank and file who would organise, and make a sacrifice of time or money, to return a candidate or control an election.

Allowing for the picturesque exaggeration of statement often thought necessary to effective journalism, there is much truth in the remark. It accounts, too, for many of the men who have come to the surface, and for not a few of the practices which have been tried under the guise of "English liberty" in the colonies and elsewhere. Lest Sir Charles Gavan Duffy should deceive himself, as well as other people, as to the true meaning of the prominence of the Irish Celts in Colonial Legislatures and Cabinets, Municipal Councils and Road Boards, I will presume to imitate his favourite practice, and relate a little anecdote, the only artistic drawback to which is that it happens to be true.

One day, walking through the great Melbourne legal hive, appropriately called Temple Court, I came upon two barrister friends—one a Celt, the other an Anglo-Saxon. The former had just been returned for some "up-country" constituency, but, as he well knew and, to do him justice, would have been the first to admit, he was in intellectual grasp or political capacity altogether the inferior of the Englishman, who saw no prospect of adding the magic letters M.P. to his name.

"Why don't you," said the glowing young Irish colonist, "stand for some country constituency? You would be sure to be returned."

"Well," said the Anglo-Saxon slowly, with a quiet smile, "I am not an Irishman, and therefore the Irish wouldn't vote for me. I *am* an Englishman, but no English elector would consider *that* any reason for giving me his support."

Here we have the gist of the matter. Whatever Lord Salisbury may think, it is really to the ambitious young colonist, emulous of public honours, in many cases a distinct misfortune to belong to the "Imperial consolidating" English race. No Australian needs the bulky book of Mr. Hogan, or the magazine essay of Sir C. Gavan Duffy, to assure him that the Irish Celt is a powerful factor for good or evil in our colonial affairs. It is as true as any such general statement can be that every Irishman is a politician,—not only a voter at elections, but an organiser and a wire-puller, and what is called the "Roman Catholic vote" has become the veritable monster of the colonial Frankenstein. Let me tell Sir C. Gavan Duffy another little colonial electioneering story, the moral of which is, I think, equally obvious.

There was to be a keen contest in one of the divisions of Melbourne, and it became known, from certain unmistakable indications, that at the eleventh hour the dreaded Roman Catholic vote had been ordered to go over to the other side. In this emergency what was to be done? On the Committee was a very enthusiastic and, of course, sharp-witted Jewish gentleman who said: "If the Irish are going to sell us, after what Father —— solemnly promised me, why shouldn't we call on the Church of England clergyman, who is not only universally respected in the constituency, but has far and away the biggest flock?"

Drowning men, especially in the sea of politics, clutch at any straw; and so a deputation waited on the worthy Canon. Fixing his genial eye on the acute physiognomy of the expectant Semite, the most influential Anglican clergyman in the district gravely said:—

"I think, gentlemen, were I to bend my mind to it, I could perhaps induce my aged and somewhat imbecile verger to vote for your man. But there is not another person I would presume to influence, on such a matter, in my parish."

Perhaps this is not an inappropriate place to point out another trait which sharply distinguishes a very worthy and not inconsiderable section of the Englishry in the colonies from the Celtic Irish. One of the most intellectual, and certainly one of the most estimable, men it has ever been my good fortune to know intimately—an old English colonist who has lived in Australia for nearly forty years, and whose judgment and opinion I would rather have on almost any mundane question than that of two-thirds of the House of Commons, to say nothing of the local Legislative Assembly—once gravely said to me:—

"I have only voted once since I have been in the colony. I voted for So-and-So; and don't know if God has forgiven me, but I certainly have not forgiven myself."

It may be urged that a political pessimist of this pronounced type, however worthy in all the private relations of life, is not fit to be a citizen of a free State. There may be some truth in this, though I remember Mr. Ruskin, who is not held to be an ignoble or unenlightened Englishman, making a very similar public confession. If, on the other hand, the principle to "poll early, and poll often," be the mark of perfect citizenhood, then I must admit that the Irish Celts attain to a very lofty standard indeed. At the same time, let me point out that under universal suffrage—of which, nevertheless, I have always been an advocate—the cultured and highly individualised type of Mr. Ruskin, and my old colonial friend, which is, in many respects, the salt of the earth, must be "bossed" by party "rings" and vulgar political "wire-pullers," whose one grand aim in life is to see that the "right name" is dropped into the slit in the ballot-box.

These illustrations are, I trust, sufficient to show the undue influence that a minority, bound together by racial and religious ties, will often exercise in an intelligent but divided community.

The best passage in Mr. Hogan's book is an eloquent extract from a lecture by Mr. James Smith, a well-known Melbourne journalist, eulogising the filial piety of the Irish domestic servants, both in America and Australia. Speaking from his own experience, Mr. Smith gives an instance of three sisters, "unsophisticated but warm-hearted Irish girls, domestic servants in this city, who regularly remit one-third of their earnings every year to Ireland in order to support an aged and widowed mother in comfort and independence." No one will deny that such "acts of filial piety" are in the highest degree praiseworthy. But Mr. Smith, with what Herbert Spencer aptly calls "the anti-patriotic bias" of the cultured Englishman, fails to see that this generous behaviour is purely tribal. The class whom he so highly eulogises, and which owes everything to Australia or America, as the case may be, is at heart essentially and narrowly

Irish. The real question is, What do the Irish in Australia contribute spontaneously to Australian or Imperial objects? I was once struck by the remark of a shrewd Scotchman as we were gazing, with admiration, on St. Patrick's Roman Catholic Cathedral, Melbourne. Said he: "Many and many a Protestant pound has found its way into those solid walls; but do you think there is a single brick in any of our churches towards which they have given a shilling?"

It is exactly the same with regard to the charitable institutions; the Roman Catholics have always received large donations from the Protestants, but given little or nothing in return. Take the memorable instance of the £95,000 sent from Australia to relieve the last Irish famine. This sum, as Mr. Hogan says, was truly magnificent for a scattered population of only 4,000,000; but to adduce it as a proof of the munificence of Irish-Australian generosity, as he does, is sheer misrepresentation or gross stupidity. To my own knowledge, large amounts were contributed by English and Scotch colonists, and I very much doubt if the Irish contributions amounted to one-third of the whole. This is just an apt illustration of the fact that the English and Scotch colonists have surmounted the merely tribal or national instincts, and when the need arises they give freely to any deserving cause. The Irish, on the other hand, despite the "filial piety" which Mr. Smith very properly belauds, are not prone to bestow their charity on non-Irish objects.

I refrain from dwelling on the darker aspects of the Irish character. Mr. Topp, quoting from Hayter's Year-Book, summarises the criminal statistics of Victoria thus: "Out of every thousand Irish-born inhabitants of the colony, 80 were arrested, of Scottish-born, 40; of English and Welsh, 26; and of Victorian natives, 11." And of "43 criminals executed during the fifteen years from 1865 to 1879, 18 were Irish-born, and 22 were Roman Catholics;" an appalling ratio, when we bear in mind that they only number altogether one-fourth of the population.

I will close this chapter by giving my reasons for considering the autonomy of Victoria and the other colonies no rule for English statesmen to go by in dealing with Ireland. I regret to find that on this subject of Irish Home Rule, I seem to be in conflict with Major-General Sir Andrew Clarke, another of that distinguished band of Anglo-Irishmen, who were chief among the Conscript Fathers of the great colony of Victoria. Sir Andrew, it is well known, contested Chatham in the interests of Mr. Gladstone's Home-Rule proposals; and I can only conceive that, judging from the great part which he and a mere handful of Anglo-Irish gentry have played in our colonial history, he thinks, with the splendid courage of his race, that they could repeat the tale on the other side of the Irish Channel. With the highest feelings of respect towards himself, I must take leave gravely to dissent from this view, and to point out that the career of Mr. Parnell, who is of his own race and creed, should be a warning rather than an example.

It cannot be too clearly asserted that there is no real analogy between the system of self-government in Victoria and the only kind of "Home Rule" possible in Ireland. *There is only one township in Victoria, a small one named Kilmore, in which there is even a bare majority of Irish Celts.* To make the case of Victoria and Ireland at all analogous, it would be necessary that Melbourne and every other large town (except one) should be at least twice as Celtic as the township of Kilmore. If Sir Andrew Clarke will try to picture such a Victoria as this, he may then be able to form some idea of the difficulty that even men like himself and Sir William Foster Stawell would have had in the early days of "responsible government" in the colony. As a matter of fact, they would have been swept into the sea.

In the course of a recent correspondence with Mr. John Bright—to whom every loyal Englishman, irrespective of mere party divisions, should feel profoundly and personally grateful—I put the case of the supposed analogy in a way that seemed to meet with his approbation. Let me quote a paragraph of my letter for the special benefit of Sir Andrew Clarke.

"In the colonies we may have strayed in some points from what you would deem true Liberalism; but in all our legislation we have proceeded on the principle that we are *one* people. Our Irish fellow-colonists, when ill-advised, clamour against this. On Mr. Gladstone's plan we should have, in the colonies, a distinct and hostile Irish Roman Catholic nationality in a generation." This, in the fewest possible words, is the answer to the tissue of fallacies which Sir C. Gavan Duffy has woven together and called an "Australian example."

As a loyal colonist I cannot close without expressing my personal weariness of—I should say, contempt for—the cheap claptrap attacks so constantly made on Great Britain—her people, her government, and her Empire. What other nation, since the world began, would have suffered to grow up, and have even fostered under her broad ægis, such a belt of self-governing republics scattered all round the habitable globe? Under whose beneficent Imperial sway but hers could we find men whose past record is of political incendiarism, if not public crime, who, on showing any disposition to hold the lamp of Civilisation in lieu of the torch of Anarchy, have been elevated to posts of supreme trust, and have had pension, place, and title showered upon them? Truly, this Victorian era of ours, at least so far as it is concerned with the great Empire of Queen Victoria, is an era of hitherto unknown toleration of every form of race, creed, and opinion. From this all-embracing, beneficent path, who would wish to return to the narrow, miry byways of the intolerant Past? Britain, and her self-governing dependencies, as well as the great nation across the Atlantic, sprung from her loins, all prayerfully desire that they may be able to keep the path of freedom and toleration. But we must bear in mind that it is an experiment, and not an assured triumph, until it is proved that by this means, a hostile race, clinging to an alien creed, may be raised and assimilated. One of our most thoughtful modern poets, in a desponding mood, describes the task as being beyond even the strength of

> "The weary Titan,
> Bearing on shoulders immense,
> Atlantëan, the load
> Wellnigh not to be borne,
> Of the too vast orb of her fate."

Our greatest living philosopher tells us that Progress is not continuous, but rhythmic, like the waves of the sea, and that there is the ebb as well as the flow. And so, underlying this much-vexed "Irish Question," we should all train ourselves to recognise one of those strong, retrogressive forces that must either destroy the Empire, or be itself destroyed; and in this light I trust that this sketch of the "Irish in Australia" is not without political significance to the English and Scottish reader.

CHAPTER VII.

THE STATE SCHOOLMASTER.

AFTER the broad fact of their democratic basis, the most general and most remarkable feature in connection with the social and political development of the Australian colonies is the general system of public education that has been adopted. Education has, in fact, been made a State Department, and is managed on strictly unsectarian, or, if you will, non-religious, lines. *Free, secular,*[1] *and compulsory,* these three words form the magic talisman that has enabled the colonial politician to overcome the opposition of the Churches and sects, each of which, it may be fairly assumed, was anxious that at least its own religious creeds and formularies should be expounded in the public schools, at the public expense.

Why, it may be asked, have these young communities been so eager to *compel* their children to be educated up to certain standards, at the cost of

[1] Not necessarily purely "secular." See Appendix E, "Education in Australia."

the general tax-payer, rather than at that of the individual parent? Why, too, if bent on this general experiment in educational socialism, should they have banished religion from the curriculum?

For the British reader to be able to grapple with these Australian problems, it is, above all things, necessary that he should keep steadily before his mind the utterly different social conditions of the two communities. None of these political problems can be solved so long as we continue to regard them as so many abstract propositions. For instance, it is absurd to argue, because we Australians declined to sanction Wentworth's scheme of creating a brand-new local peerage, that we are all bent on destroying that venerable institution in the mother country. Personally I read the felicitous speech of Lord Balfour of Burleigh, the other day, welcoming the Marquis of Salisbury to Edinburgh, with an historical relish that was heightened by the associations called forth by the high-sounding names of host and guest. But I should only be struck with a sense of the incongruous and the ridiculous in Mr. Smith of Melbourne, or Mr. Brown of Sydney, being suddenly converted into Earls or Marquises. This matter of titles, which is after all a minor matter, furnishes,

THE STATE SCHOOLMASTER 159

I think, a not inapt illustration of the sociological differences between Great Britain and Australia.

Before proceeding any further with my subject of the "State Schoolmaster," let me frankly say that under the utterly different social conditions of England, a very large number of thoughtful "Australian secularists" would, if they transferred their residence to this country, be warm supporters of the "voluntary" or religious schools working in conjunction with the Board Schools under Mr. Forster's great Act. In England there is a fairly homogeneous people, possessing a Church and a religious system of education, that, by reason of its influence, extent, and antiquity, is entitled to be called "national." "Of the 15,000 voluntary schools," says the Rev. Dr. Rigg, a prominent but honourably fair-minded Wesleyan, "not less than 12,000 belong to the Church of England." To recklessly use the tax-payers' money for the wanton destruction of these voluntary schools, and for the substitution, regardless of cost, of a purely secular system, seems to me, as an Australian secularist, the height of folly, and the result not of enlightenment, but of sectarian bitterness, envy, and animosity.

But we in Australia have to begin our "nation-building" at the very beginning. We are not a homogeneous people. So great in numbers is the Irish minority that we are veritably two races. On the matter of religion, we have been compelled to organise the State on a basis of indifference—so various and antagonistic are the religious divisions of the people.

To come now to the question of the national systems of education in Australia, I would point out that the present unsectarian or non-religious system has simply superseded the old "denominational" or religious system which was first tried in all the colonies and, judged by the test of the ballot-box, pronounced a dismal and universal failure. I can speak from personal experience of the denominational system in Victoria, before the passing of Mr. Wilberforce Stephen's Education Act. Whilst the general run of the Protestant schools were fairly efficient, and assisted in some measure to fit the future citizen to play his part in a free and, what should therefore be, an enlightened community, the Roman Catholic schools were universally acknowledged to be the worst in the land. I have known pious parents of that faith constantly in danger of the priestly ban for the crime of removing their children from their own schools, where their education was being ne-

THE STATE SCHOOLMASTER 161

glected, to others, where it would be looked after with some degree of efficiency. Of course, it may be said that it is no concern of the State if a certain section of the people are willing to submit to an inefficient system of schooling for their sons and daughters.

It was on this ground, I believe, that the two former Anglican Bishops of Melbourne, Dr. Perry and Dr. Moorhouse, were both advocates of the Roman Catholic claims. But there is another, and to my mind much more important, side to the question. Is any State—least of all a democratic State—in a condition of stability when one-fourth of its members on all vital points, except that of a common language, remains alien? I do not know any writer who has put this side of the question with such force as Mr. Topp, and I will therefore quote a few sentences from his essay on "English Institutions and the Irish Race:"—

"It is not too much to say that the assimilation of the Irish is the first necessity to every English community. Fortunately, we in Victoria have a means to our hand which, though not consciously devised for this purpose, is partially adapted to effect it. This is the Education Act. By means of it, the youth of the Roman Catholic population is

L

gradually passed through the State Schools, and, mixing, as it therefore does, with the young of other sects, it must inevitably cease to retain any strong feeling of bigotry or exclusiveness. . . . The Education Act may be defective in many respects, and is undoubtedly a great expense to the community. It may even be thought by *doctrinaires* to be going altogether beyond the proper functions of the State. But if, in the course of a generation, it enables us to eliminate a baneful and corrupting influence, no cost that may be paid for it can be considered too great. . . . Should it be objected that the views here propounded are indicative of religious bigotry and a non-recognition of the doctrine of toleration, it can be answered that there is something more important even than toleration, and that is the peace and happiness of the people. Before toleration can work beneficially for any community, all its members must have attained a certain uniform level of intelligence and morality; otherwise the toleration is all on one side. The less advanced part of the community gets the benefit of it, without having either the desire or the ability to reciprocate."—(*Melbourne Review*, Jan. 1881.)

THE STATE SCHOOLMASTER 163

Although the constituencies have supported this system of "free, secular, and compulsory" education everywhere in Australia by decisive majorities, the battle still rages, and a determined opposition, mainly by the Roman Catholic clergy, is kept up, against the Education Act. It is significant, however, that the bulk of their flocks show very little, if any, real hostility to the system. I have recently felt it my duty to read almost a roomful of controversial writings on this education question in Australia. By far the most intelligent advocate I have met of the Roman Catholic demands for a separate public grant for their schools is Mr. Charles Fairfield, who puts the issues with great clearness, from his standpoint, in an essay entitled "Those Catholic Claims" (*Melbourne Review*, Jan. 1885). When confronted with the low standard of general education displayed in all countries where his co-religionists have had the matter entirely in their own hands, Mr. Fairfield, with engaging frankness, confesses that if asked, "What sort of workmanship do Catholics turn out in countries such as Spain, where they have still very much their own way in educational matters, or in Italy, where they formerly had?" his plain answer would be, "Well, one can't say much for it! The reason why they have bad schools in Spain is because nearly every other institution of the country is three parts rotten."

If we would see the denominational system worked to real advantage by the Roman Catholics, Mr. Fairfield thinks we should turn to England. "The reason why the Catholic schools in England," he remarks, "are models of efficiency, discipline, and good order, is because all the other social and political institutions surrounding them are in good trim. So that Catholic elementary schools, *plus* English civilisation, are worth having; and Catholic elementary schools without the stimulus of rival systems, and without the bracing atmosphere of the best modern civilisations, are not up to much. . . . I know that some Catholics would go through anything rather than acknowledge that their educators borrow from the culture or the civilisation that surrounds them. But never mind that; they do. With shocking inconsistency, some of them have a positive knack of borrowing and assimilating the best educational methods of their rivals. In England, Catholics are 'on their good behaviour.' For many years they

THE STATE SCHOOLMASTER 165

have had, in face of a community, modern, enlightened, critical, and suspicious, to justify their existence."

This, as I understand it, is to declare that in Spain, where the system is practically supreme, the general education is deplorable, while in England, where the Roman Catholics form a small and, so far as the purely English element is concerned, an exceptional minority, they are on "their good behaviour," and kept up to the mark.[1] Can any admission be more damaging? But in dealing with the results of the Roman Catholic schools under the old denominational system in Victoria, we were unfortunately confronted with a state of things more like that of Spain than that of England. Had the Roman Catholic schools in the colony been at all up even to the very ordinary Protestant standard, I very gravely doubt whether the community would have disturbed them; most

---

[1] The English criminal statistics, however, tell a less flattering tale.—"The actual results range from fifteen, twenty, and forty per cent., up to gaols (as in Liverpool) where the Roman Catholic prisoners are considerably in excess of all others confined. In two great cities the Roman Catholic female prisoners have for several years averaged three times the numbers of the remainder of their sex."—*Quarterly Review*, January 1888, p. 60.

certainly the present enormously costly system would never have been attempted.

In the very next number of the periodical, in which Mr. Fairfield pleaded for the Roman Catholic claims, Sir Robert Stout, the late Premier of New Zealand, in an article entitled "Our Waifs and Strays," subjected the whole question to the crushing test of statistics. Sir Robert Stout, I may remark, is one of the very few prominent public men in Australasia who is an open disbeliever in Christianity. His article therefore should be perused with caution, as it is quite impossible, especially for a capable man, to take up so exceptional and so hostile an attitude against the bulk of his fellows, and not display an "anti-religious bias." Sir Robert Stout attempts to show by figures (1) that the churches that are loudest in denouncing secular education have the worst record; and (2) that "godless" schools have not produced so many wicked children as the sectarian seminaries. I do not question the accuracy of his statistics; but I draw a different inference from them. Mr. Hayter, the Government Statist of Victoria, has a very pithy way of summing up the vital statistics of that colony. From 1865 to 1876, he tells us, there were forty-one criminals executed, of whom not one was born in Victoria;—so it is clear that the State schools cannot be held responsible in any of these cases. Of this number, two only were natives of other Australian colonies; there were nine Englishmen, one Welshman, seventeen Irishmen, two Scotchmen; and for Belgium, France, Switzerland, United States, and West Indies, one each; China, four; at sea, one. Twelve of these forty-one claimed to be of the Church of England, twenty-one were Roman Catholics, two Presbyterians, three Wesleyans, and three Pagans. Thirty-six were cases of murder, and the residue capital cases of other kinds. As I have elsewhere pointed out, these figures are the more startling, when it is borne in mind that the Roman Catholics only number a fourth of the population.

These statistics, published from year to year, by Mr. Hayter, have really furnished the most powerful argument in favour of the State schools, and against the old system of giving large grants to the various religious denominations for educational purposes. But, as I have said, while bound to accept such statistics, I by no means draw the anti-religious deductions from them so trenchantly set forth by Sir Robert Stout. He appears to argue that crimes prevail among certain classes *because* of their religious belief; instead of, as I prefer to think, *in spite* of it. I hold that the great majority of human beings would be far worse citizens, as well as far more unhappy creatures, if deprived of their religious faith, and their supernatural aspirations. As I have said at the beginning of the chapter, I should be an advocate for religious education in the State schools in Australia, but for the fact that the people are so sharply divided into two races, which can only be assimilated by a common system of national education. In addition to this there is no religious communion like the Anglican Church in England, which, by its numbers, wealth, and *prestige*, could carry on the education of the country on religious lines, to the satisfaction of even a bare majority of the people. It was the hopelessness of the task in these new countries to make the State teach religion that has impelled so many religious men, and in fact the great majority of a not irreligious community, to favour the secular system. To show that my own position is not a singular or isolated one, I may point out that from the days of Sir Richard Bourke and Robert Lowe, in New South

Wales to those of the late Wilberforce Stephen,[1] in Victoria, many of the most distinguished members of the Anglican laity, despite their Bishops, have been among the chief supporters of the national, as opposed to the denominational, system of education. In fact, remembering that Mr. Higinbotham—in my opinion, the real father of the system in Victoria, though Mr. Stephen framed and carried the measure through Parliament—was then at least, also a prominent churchman, it may be said that the present State schools are largely the creation of the enlightened laity of Dr. Moorhouse's communion.

But to my mind there is a much more imperative argument in favour of the State, or, as they were first called, Common, schools, than any to be derived from Mr. Hayter's criminal statistics. Let me digress for a moment to observe that the term Common schools was a really more felicitous one than State schools, for it emphasised the main point that they were intended to be "common" to every church, sect, and social class in the community—

---

[1] The late eminent Victorian lawyer and judge, then Attorney-General for the colony, who framed and passed the present Education Act of Victoria.

in other words, to be broadly and truly National. But stupid parents did not like the idea of their children going to "common" schools, and associating with common children, so the name, with its grand significance, was sacrificed to that vulgar snobbishness which is just as rampant in democracies as elsewhere. These fastidious Australians would, I presume, had they been consulted, have changed the "Book of Common Prayer" into the "Volume of Polite Supplication;" and the "House of Commons," translated into their nomenclature, would have become the "Assembly of Genteels." Let us, however, pass on from the mere name to the thing itself. In my opinion, the full justification, as well as the immediate cause, of the free, secular, and compulsory system of public education now in vogue in Australia, is the hostile attitude assumed by the Roman Catholic clergy towards the rest of the community, as shown by their persistent efforts to isolate and divide their flocks from it. From time to time the leading Roman Catholic prelates of Australia have fulminated against what are called "mixed marriages!" but, whatever the evil of these mixed marriages may be, it is quite evident that unless they take place there can never be a united and homogeneous people in the land. In the course of this book I have more than once had occasion to refer to Scotland as affording the most happy illustration of the successful blending of two originally hostile races. But suppose the Highlanders as a body had been Roman Catholics, and had been forbidden, under dire ecclesiastical anathemas, to marry with the Lowlanders, what would be the condition of Scotland at the present day? Now, this is the state of things that the Australians, on the very threshold of their existence as a people, have to face. So long as the Irish-Australian flocks slavishly obey their priests, there must be this great bar and division between what I have called the two races in Australia. But if, as Mr. Topp points out, we can bring the young Irish-Australian children into the State schools, to be trained and educated side by side with the children of more enlightened parents, there may be some hope in a generation or two of raising that section of the community to the necessary level of the prevailing civilisation, whence will follow their complete fusion into the future Australian people.

For good or evil, this free, secular, and compulsory system has been established. Let us, instead of indulging in the futile abuse or equally futile laudation of the measure, impose upon ourselves the worthier task of endeavouring to find out what are its real aims, and what are its probable results. I cannot think of a better way to assist the British reader in this enterprise than by giving him a life-like picture of a lofty type of the Victorian State schoolmaster, which came into my hands under the following circumstances.

When the Great Melbourne Exhibition was held in 1880, among the Government exhibits was the model of an "up-country" State school, with all the fittings and appliances used in the daily routine of educational work. This, however, was only the shell; but the kernel, in the form of a somewhat undersized "bush" schoolmaster, sat inside. With that feeling of contempt which all metropolitans seem to have for country-folk, and which, as Prince Bismarck observes, is a sign of their own frothy imbecility, we Melbournians were at first disposed to ignore this "live exhibit" who insisted at intervals on explaining the aim and scope of public education, especially as applied to the inland towns and remote bush villages of Victoria. We soon discovered that it was not possible to ignore him for long. He had lived among his rude urchins and the lonesome gum-trees so long that the throng and bustle of the city, and the voices of so many people, with at least a smattering of culture, seemed to set his brain on fire. For he had read widely and pondered deeply in his bush solitudes, and had not only the phrases of the philosophers on his tongue, but their profoundest and most suggestive thoughts in his mind. And now here were numbers of other men with varying experiences and opinions, with whom for the first time he could converse freely on these high themes. He had an odd way of speaking about celebrated personages, as though he knew them intimately, and would say: "I like Thomas immensely, though I often find him very crotchety; but when I want a thoroughly rational chum, give me Herbert;"—and it took one rather aback to realise that his familiar bush companions were the authors of *Sartor Resartus* and *First Principles*.

On a closer acquaintance, it transpired that the young "up-country" schoolmaster, whose name was Charles Wesley Caddy,[1] had beguiled his leisure by

---

[1] The sad intelligence has just reached me that this really gifted man was recently run over by a cab in Melbourne and killed.

putting some of his reflections into literary form. It then became evident that the bush-student, unlike the city smatterers, was not only acquainted with the luminous philosophy of our day, based on the Theory of Evolution, but could explain and quaintly illustrate its far-reaching truths by apt illustrations drawn from our everyday common colonial life. We at least could find him a vehicle for such rare effusions, and so, scattered amongst the newspapers and periodicals of the day, may be found such perfect essays of their kind as " The Morals of Politics," " The Education of the Educated," " The Belief of Unbelievers," all richly deserving preservation in book-form. Imbedded in one of these essays, by Mr. Wesley Caddy, was a personal sketch of a Victorian country schoolmaster, which, throwing light as it does on this great controversy of sectarian *versus* secular education, I here transcribe in part :—

"There died at Daylesford, a few months ago, a gentleman who had been in the service of the Victorian Education Department for many years; and who, with two or three other noted teachers, had been selected for an inspectorship of schools. He died before the time fixed for the commencement of his new duties. His career has been favourably noticed by every Government inspector who had gauged his work and noted his methods of instruction. Like all enthusiasts, he reckoned nothing small that related to his own art. He reduced the 'result-grinding' to a science, and year after year made his scholars pass a better examination than was done in any other Victorian school. He knew how to make a school pay. These were the points in which he excelled in following the work of education as a business; and if this was all that could be said of him, there would be no reason for dwelling on his career any more than on that of a successful shopkeeper. But he had, and contrived to instil into other teachers, the conviction that teaching was a great art. To bring on a crop of youngsters vying with each other in their school work, and to cultivate in them a love of fairplay and a detestation of everything mean and low, was the delight of his life. He knew the value of ritual as a controlling power over children, as well as some sections of religious teachers know its efficacy in managing childlike men. A boy sent to him by an assistant and charged with an offence, was dealt with in a manner as solemn as that assumed by a

Supreme Court judge. No criminal guilty of manslaughter ever felt the enormity of his offence more keenly than that boy when the consequences to himself and younger boys were pointed out of acting in a dishonourable manner; and the boy always left the room convinced of the justice of his punishment and the sinfulness of his offence."

. . . . . .

Children draw their general notions of religious obligation from the family and from Sunday-school teachings; but their code of honour is picked up at school. In a large State school of 800 children, such as that of which the late Geddie Pearse was head teacher, the number of children who can be dealt with individually by the head teacher is necessarily small. The work of the head teacher in such a case will be to try and impress his methods on his assistants. And where a large staff can be got to follow up such methods in dealing with the morals of children, no man can deny that the greatest possible amount of moral culture is being obtained. What Geddie Pearse achieved in Daylesford and elsewhere is being daily attempted in hundreds of Victorian schools. There are, of course, numbers of teachers who have no higher idea of their work than that it is, according to their position in the service, a good or bad occupation as a money-making affair; and who, if they can get their scholars to show up creditably at the annual examinations, consider they have delivered their souls. But the number of these bears probably about the same ratio to the number of those who are solicitous about conduct as well as attainments, as the number of money-grubbing clergymen bears to the number of those really desirous of promoting the spread of purity of life. That is to say, the work of moral instruction is being as well carried out under our strictly secular system as the work of religious instruction is being carried out in the churches; and the bulk of the people are now so well satisfied of this that, unless the clergy and their organs cease their clamour against the good work notoriously being done in large towns and in out-of-the-way bush hamlets, the respect and support accorded from traditional usage to the pastoral office will be withdrawn, and given to the class which is really furthering the spread of enlightenment.

One would fain close with this pleasant little sketch of the model Australian schoolmaster—this Roger Ascham of the Bush, who expended his life and thoughts, and gave up his days and nights, to his schoolful of colonial children, as faithfully as did his predecessor to Queen Elizabeth and the one or two favoured ladies of her Court. But it is as well to thresh this subject out thoroughly, and to see the dark side and the dangers as well as the brilliant successes of the system. It is not denied, even by its most enthusiastic advocates, that the free, secular, and compulsory system of education cannot be established in any country without a considerable national outlay. Could a race of headmasters of the type of Geddie Pearse be always found, no expense would be too great. But of course such a man in any profession or walk of life is the exception rather than the rule. The question then is, does the system work sufficiently well to justify the outlay in such communities as our colonies?

I think that any impartial person who has actually studied the subject on the spot will be almost sure to answer in the affirmative. In the first place, I would beg the British reader not to be misled by such phrases as "godless" education, as applied to the Australian State schools. So misleading are all such epithets that

I confess, friend as I am of the State schools, I was astonished to find how essentially religious the teaching is in the authorised reading-books, or "Royal Readers," as they are called in Victoria. I thought that even Mr. Alexander Sutherland, the well-known graduate of the Melbourne University, a foremost authority on education, as well as a capable and copious writer mainly on local historical matters, might have unconsciously over-stated this fact in his controversy with the Victorian clergy who are always agitating for the repeal of the Act. I find, however, from an examination of these Victorian school-books that he is to a great extent justified in his assertion that they are "saturated with religion;" and so, he adds, "are the ordinary instructions of the teachers."

What, then, can be the grievance of the clergy— Roman Catholic or Protestant? Frankly, it is, so far as they do oppose the Education Act, that the teachers are forbidden to give any religious—which under the circumstances must be sectarian—teaching in school hours.[1] Can it be otherwise in a mixed community where all religions are tolerated and none are favoured? This, I feel quite con-

[1] See Appendix E, "Education in Australia."

vinced, is the common-sense view of the question taken by that powerful potentate in a democracy, the working-class elector. He is of opinion that the State school system should have a much more extended, and, he would add, a much fairer, trial than it has yet received. I think that the majority of the Protestant clergy are beginning to realise this, and it is only fair to say that many of them were from the first active and unwearying promoters of it. This applies without doubt to the more earnest of the Wesleyans, Independents, Baptists, and the leaders of the other sects styled in England Dissenters.

But it does not appear to be the case so widely with the Anglicans or the Presbyterians, particularly the former, which I attribute, so far as Victoria is concerned, to the deservedly great influence of the first two Bishops of Melbourne who were both avowed opponents of so-called secular education. Writing from an admittedly political point of view, I venture to express a hope that the leaders of the Colonial Church of England will carefully reconsider their position. These nascent nations are just now at the great turning-point of their career. In which direction their future lies, rests with Fate. But of this I am sure: the majority of thinking persons—for it is a mistake to suppose that the colonial working-classes do not think—have resolutely made up their minds, whatever the immediate cost may be, to weld the various races admitted into the commonwealth of the great Island-Continent into one people. It is the only way to change a condition of things that might almost be described as a chronic state of civil war. The majority of the people see this plainly enough, and through that too often shaky and babbling mouthpiece, the politician, they have handed over the work to the State schoolmaster. Many of the clergy not unnaturally regard this bold act as an infraction of their rights, but let them remember that it need not be so if they are wise. This may read like a paradox, but it is a plain fact.

The people of Australia are quite as religious as the people of England. They will, however, instinctively turn to those religious teachers who are prepared to assist and not to thwart the essential educational movement intended to make them, as far as possible, a united and a homogeneous people. Speaking again with perhaps unpardonable boldness, I venture to assert that if the Anglican Church in Australia should develop at the critical moment a man of genius as its chief priest and leader, he will entirely reverse the policy of his great predecessors from Bishop Broughton to Bishop Moorhouse. What benefit has accrued to that Church from the powerful assistance it has rendered to the Roman Catholics in opposition to the State schools? None; except it be to "dis-Australianise" herself. If a man of the commanding ability and restless energy of Dr. Moorhouse could not stem the tide, what hope is there for a lesser man? Instead of opposing the State school system which is the inevitable outcome of the social condition of the country, how much wiser it would be for the Anglicans and Presbyterians, whose zeal, learning, and piety are widely recognised and revered, to assist to widen the school curriculum, and to aid instead of thwart the State schoolmaster.

Had such men as Bishop Perry and Bishop Moorhouse, from the first, countenanced this essential educational reform, whereby Victorian children were to go to school "in common" at the public expense, they could have demanded a just compromise on the subject of religion, and caused to be brought into force a measure similar to the Public Instruction Act of 1880, which Sir Henry Parkes introduced into New South Wales. So long as they had supported a "Common" system of public education—"free" and "compulsory"—the people would not have insisted on its being "secular." They, in fact, only did so in despair, finding it impossible to get the religious leaders to do anything but blindly oppose what their own instinct of self-preservation told them was essential to the salvation of the State. Had the two worthy and eminent prelates I have named cordially supported the movement, they could have dictated their own terms as to the State school curriculum, and they would have earned the undying gratitude of all right-thinking patriotic men in the colonies, and would have done much, without the change by a hair's-breadth of an article or formulary of their creed, to make their Church the Church of Australia.

It may not unnaturally be asked by an attentive English student of Australian affairs, whether this system of free, secular, and compulsory education is not likely, sooner or later, to be overthrown. The fact that a large and organised minority, controlled by vigilant ecclesiastical leaders, is opposed to the State schools, is certainly a fact not to be overlooked or lightly considered. I will frankly concede that

I have always considered it quite possible that the opponents of the State schools may, in one or other of these colonies, succeed in snatching a chance victory in a corrupt or moribund legislature. I remember discussing the possibility with a very far-seeing colonial politician, to whom I quoted the excellent American phrase to the effect that "persistent bigotry is, in the long-run, more than a match for wobbling enlightenment." With a long knowledge of Australian public affairs gained in and out of Parliament, my friend replied somewhat after this fashion :—

"Suppose," he said, "for the sake of argument, that it is granted there may be a chance majority who will vote the re-establishment of denominational schools in our colony. You will admit that it is not very likely to occur, and could not possibly occur, if the issues were put fairly before the people. Such a blow at the State school system, therefore, could only be the result of a chance majority in what would be a very corrupt, and by no means representative, House. What would follow after this alarming division when the appeal to the electors took place? Do you think the people, having literally studded the land with State schools, are going to destroy them, and revert to the old inefficient anti-national system? No; mark my words, the only result of such an unlikely contingency as you predict would be the immediate return of an overwhelming majority pledged to their eyes to re-establish, without a moment's delay, the State schools. And to make sure that no such retrograde movement should ever again take place, I make no doubt that a much more aggressive measure would be passed, under which no person should be allowed to hold any post or office in the State who had not been trained in the State schools."

I will conclude this sketch of the State schoolmaster by offering a few remarks concerning his aristocratic relative, the University Professor. The Universities, like the State schools, are secular institutions; but their education is certainly not free, —neither is it compulsory. The fees are heavy, and the students limited. Despite the fact that Australian Universities owe their origin to the far-seeing political genius of Wentworth, and that throughout Australia these institutions have been favoured with an exceptionally capable professoriate, I think that *alma mater* is still somewhat of an aristocratic exotic in these democratic colonies. The fault seems to be that we have striven too slavishly to imitate the great English models; or rather, I should say, the Colonial Universities have not moved with the times, and are now, from a popular standpoint, altogether behind the "Home" Universities. This, however, is a subject on which I will not presume to dogmatise, but considering its bearing on the general subject of Australian education, I will venture to append the opinion of one who can speak with some show of authority.[1] I allude to Professor Herbert A. Strong, now of Victoria University, Liverpool, who a short time ago vacated the Classical Professorship in the University of Melbourne, but whose warmest sentiments are still with the people of that great colony in which he passed an important portion of his life. In answer to certain questions on the subject which I recently submitted to him, Professor Strong remarks: "My idea of the Melbourne University is that it is doing a great and noble work there. The fault of its curriculum is the absence of modern languages and of real philology teaching. It is (or was five years ago) behind in its physiology. The Universities here have much more effect upon the

[1] See Appendix E, "Education in Australia."

masses, because the professors do not think it *infra dig.* to lecture to the people at large, and to try and do for England what the Scotch professors have done for Scotland."

In my opinion, this is not creditable to the chief educational institution of a democratic community which supports it out of the public revenue by a grant of £9000 annually. Yet the Melbourne University undoubtedly still holds the supreme place in the public mind, mainly, no doubt, on account of the great attainments and high reputation of its original professorial Board. But it is impossible for any institution, especially in these young democratic lands, to survive long on tradition alone. The next scene in the educational drama of Victoria will probably be the popularising of the University as the head of the State school system, and, strange as the phrase may sound in Australian ears, the modernising of its curriculum.

CHAPTER VIII.

NATIVE AUSTRALIANS AND IMPERIAL FEDERATION.

IN one of his charming after-dinner speeches recently delivered in Australia, the Earl of Carnarvon, pleasantly paraphrasing the Laureate, was good enough to say that, "if fifty years of Europe are, in point of development and expansion, worth an unlimited era of Cathay, then I say that ten years in these great Australasian colonies match fifty years of Europe."

This truth was borne in upon me very forcibly when I took up one of the later numbers of the now unfortunately defunct *Melbourne Review*, in order to find out, if I might, what "Young Australia" was thinking about himself and the Empire of which he is at present a unit. The article to which I wish to allude is entitled "Australia for the Australians," and is one of a series by a young Victorian, who writes with a certain crude ability and much self-confidence, which it is to be hoped for his own peace of mind he may retain, even though his views may ripen as the years roll on. How far the positive opinions expressed in these immature essays are representative of the opinions of the rising generation of native Australians, it is perhaps impossible to determine. But I make no doubt that a goodly percentage of the members of such a body as the "Australian Natives Association" will re-echo these sentiments, if only for the purpose of annoying their fathers. Under the circumstances, and lest I should be accused of misrepresentation, I think it advisable to allow the writer of "Australia for the Australians" to state his own case.

"The census returns for 1881 are eloquent on the point that Victoria is rapidly becoming Victorian—that is, peopled by men and women of Victorian birth. Mr. Hayter estimated that the colonial-born population in Victoria on April 3d, 1881, numbered 539,060, and the "foreigners," or British-born, 282,339; that is to say, during the previous decade between one-seventh and one-eighth of the British population disappeared. Three in every five persons in Victoria at present are colonials."

In these words the "Australian native" opens what he intends shall be a very original and startling discourse, and then with much complacency, not to say joviality, proceeds to point out how in an increasing ratio the colonial-born will "supply the places of their fathers, who will vanish before the tooth of Time." He then lays down a series of sweeping generalisations or sociological dogmas, relative to the new national type of humanity now coming into existence in Australia. These racial speculations, I must frankly confess, read to me like an odd mixture of the phraseology of *First Principles* and the ideas of *Alice in Wonderland*. The coming Australian is to enter upon the stage freed from all the wretched *impedimenta* of the historic past. His advent is to mark an entirely new era. When he takes over his patrimony, Australia, from his father, the "foreigner," the astonished Old World will see something very like a new revelation upon this earth. Here is his glorious vision of himself in his future public capacity as political lord and master of the great island-continent.

"Knowing, therefore, that the interest of the few is the robbery of the many, the Australian will sternly repress log-rolling and swindling, and will only vote for the man who will represent general, and not individual and clique, interests. He will be influenced only by a public-spirited desire for the advancement of his native land, and not for the advancement of any particular statesman or party. The legislation of the future will be the reflex of educated patriotic electors, and they will only join one party, and that will carry the Australian flag and keep step to Australian music."

"Australians," he continues, with increasing self-appreciation, "are not hindered in their search for truth by the ivy-grown traditions of past ages. Common sense and education invite them to think freely for themselves; and they are accustomed to boldly investigate everything—past, present, and future. Nothing is too sacred merely because it is hoary and fossilised. Guided by truth, they tread down the corn of established opinions, separating the chaff from the grain, appropriating the portion their judgment approves, and rejecting whatever savours of darkness and ignorance."

If this is not enough to make the Pope tremble in the Vatican, and even disconcert the Archbishop of Canterbury, whatever may be his Grace's views on the right of private judgment, I know not what is. But the panorama of the forthcoming antipodean Utopia continues unrolling before our astonished eyes:—

" It is a magnificent period in the history of humanity, a very golden age; an age of glorious innovations, full of reforms, inventions, and revolutions, when men are emerging from darkness into light, from night into day. What has been accomplished is splendid, but what has to be done is sublime; and if the colonies would not lag behind in the race, their destinies must be controlled by men saturated with the comprehension of their sacred duties, and actuated by a burning desire for the elevation of their fellows, so that the race will receive an impetus in the struggle for perfection more powerful than anything it has yet received. Our modes of thought are becoming better every year, and we are discarding superstition and employing science, because we are accustomed to pass established opinions through the alembic of reason which a scientific age has moulded for us. . . . The rising generation has been nurtured under a new and dry light, mental and moral, while the old and decaying one was forced in a hothouse of falsity. Evolution promises that we shall be better thinkers and workers than our predecessors, and the dispassionate observer must admit that my proposition that Australia will never be properly governed till she is ruled by *native*-born (*sic*) Australians has after all more of a real than a hypothetical basis. Then will our destinies be in the hands of men who will be influenced only by a sincere and creditable *amor patriæ*, whose united cry may be earnestly resounded from York to Otway, from Perth to Brisbane—Australia for the Australians!"

Let us pause for a moment to take breath. It does not appear to strike the young enthusiast how oddly these old-world names sound in his new-world peroration. How much more effective it would have been if instead of York, that outlying peninsula had been named Croajingalong, and in lieu of Perth, the name had been, for instance, that of Sydney's populous suburb, Woolloomoolloo. Even then he would have been saddled with the old-world nomenclature of a cape named after an English naval officer, and a city after an old Scottish Governor of New South Wales. But surely this very initial incongruity in the matter of new-world nomenclature should have taught him the absurdity of imagining that it is possible to establish in Australia or elsewhere an entirely new form of civilisation. The ever-lengthening, though often imperceptible, link that connects all the ages can never be broken.

It seems almost an anti-climax, but perhaps I should remark that the future Australian is to be both a "Free-trader" and an "Atheist," which strikes one as singular, remembering that the essayist's fellow-colonists are at least professedly pious, and most undeniably Protectionist. Having, however, formed my own opinion of this literary effusion, I could not help wondering what some of the genuine old pioneers of the colony would have to say to it— the men who, despite this Sir Thomas More in short clothes, had planted the seeds of civilisation in these far-off sunny southern lands where they had built their home, and made the wilderness to blossom as the rose. I had not long to wait. After a due interval there came to hand a new number of the same salmon-coloured *Review*, containing an article by an old colonist who administered severe chastisement, more in sorrow than in anger, to the youthful visionary. With fine effect the older man began by recalling a memorable passage in the *Aryan Household* of Dr. Hearn—by far the greatest philosophical work yet written in Australia. In that passage the learned and profound writer observes that the "three hundred" who, at the cost of certain death, held the pass of Thermopylæ "were all of them fathers with sons living."

"According to modern notions," adds Dr. Hearn, "a forlorn hope would naturally be composed of men who had not given hostages to fortune. Such, however, was not the light in which the matter presented itself to the Greek mind. The human plant had flowered, and the continuance of the house was secure. It was therefore of comparatively little moment what befell the man whose duty to his ancestors had been fulfilled."

After quoting this singularly suggestive passage, the old Pioneer points out to the Native Australian that his desire to push the old race into the grave is, after all, but a reversion to the usages of the antique world. "Unlike his mythic forefathers, however," he adds, "the 'Young Australian' is not at all inclined to the practice of burying his departed parent beneath the hearthstone and worshipping his spirit."

"We old Australians," continues the worthy Pioneer, "are 'foreigners'—trespassers on the land that we have given to our sons. Our intellects are 'stunted as the feet of a Chinese dame,' and, says our cruel critic, ' despite their time-honoured boast of absolute freedom, many of our fathers actually did not know what freedom was till they came hither'! How the young cockerel crows! And how we crowed too when the down was on our lips, and we felt that our certain mission was to set the whole world straight. In those days 'Young England' was as fierce and as self-confident as 'Young Australia' is in these, and possibly felt as much contempt for the old fogeys who had made England arbitress of Europe, and first in arts and arms."

Point by point does the old colonist meet and confute the youth. How, he wants to know, can the old decaying generation, with its "hothouse of falsity," have possibly produced such brilliant successors ? " The usual fruits of decay," he remarks, with a knowledge evidently not merely theoretical, " are mushrooms, or more frequently poisonous fungi. In which of these somewhat low organisms shall we class our coming rulers ?"

The writer clearly shows that he has been ruffled, but his reproof is dignified, not petulant. Young Australia had pointed with youthful conceit, rather than manly pride, to the high state of general education in Victoria. Brides and bridegrooms who signed their names with a cross in the register are fewer there than elsewhere. "For this happy state of things," cuttingly remarks the old Pioneer, "we are of course indebted to the scholars, not to the teachers—who are chiefly 'foreigners'—nor to those who established and have administered our educational system, and who certainly belonged to the decaying generation."

I have perhaps already quoted sufficient to indicate to the intelligent English reader the general drift of this, to me, most interesting discussion. The Young (native) Australian, like the greatest of living poets in *his* youth, had, as we have seen, "dipped into the future far as human eye could see;" and perhaps, if one may be allowed to say so, somewhat further. The old Pioneer, after the pathetic manner of men who have turned the solemn side of fifty, prefers to look in the opposite direction.

"Surely this young Victorian forgets that to the unwearying energy, the strong self-reliance, the clear heads and stout arms of her early settlers, his country owes the very wealth and culture of which he boasts, and to the growth of which he and his fellows have yet contributed so little! Step by step the wild lands have been reclaimed; stone by stone the noble cities built; mile by mile the far-reaching lines of rail and wire have been stretched; foot by foot the buried treasures sought and found; one by one the schools of art and learning erected and endowed. By whom? Not by the 'Young Australian,' surely! Did that freedom, which he boasts as his, spring self-begotten from the earth? Was that noble educational system which he praises born of the soil? Have the grand gifts which the fast-vanishing generation of 'foreigners' will bequeath to their sons dropped from the clear Australian skies? The gifts of art and science, of learning and culture, of commerce and manufactures, of ripening harvests and glittering ores; the shady groves of 'Academe'; the gathered treasures of literature and of the sister arts; the temples of religion and of justice; the palaces of commerce, and the huge piles that quiver to the throbbing pulses of the tireless giant whose hot breath and iron sinews obey the master's slightest touch; the parks and gardens; and the thousand homes of comfort and of health; —are all these nothing in the eyes of those of our race who are so soon to fill our vacant places? Do our sons owe us no better guerdon than this sneer at our rapidly diminishing numbers—at our early and bitter struggles? Not so is kept the memory of the fathers of the Great Republic, to be able to claim whose ancestry is to be 'the heir of all the ages in the foremost files of time.'"

Surely this proud, but far from boastful, retrospect is more moving than all the crude previsions of youth. I have frankly stated that it seems to me impossible to ascertain how far the opinions expressed in "Australia for the Australians" are the evanescent views of individual immaturity, and how far they are the day-dreams of the rising generation. I find in other numbers of the same colonial magazine, the writer was allowed space for "An Australian Protest against Imperial Federation." This essay, in my judgment, is much more worthy of the consideration of grown men, whether English or colonial, than is the cheap rhodomontade of "Australia for the Australians." If the writer may be accepted in any sense as a mouth-piece of the rising (or should it be *arisen?*) generation, then the colonial-born voters, into whose hands such questions as those involved in Imperial

Federation will be placed, are very emphatically opposed to any scheme that will bind them into closer legislative union with England. Before entering upon this subject, I would warn my readers not to imagine, because they see the crudity or, if they will, the folly of this unknown colonial writer, whom I have treated as typical of the intelligent native Australian, that those to whom he more directly appeals will read his pages with their eyes. It is worse than idle for grown-up serious men to continue to play a game of political blind man's buff, when it is admitted on all hands that the relations between Great Britain and her colonies are in a tentative, if not unsatisfactory and even critical, condition. Surely we should endeavour to remove the bandages of ignorance and conventionality, so as to see one another in our true aspect.

I propose to devote the remaining pages of this chapter to the consideration of the very complex problem of the relations between the mother country and her colonies. It is a singular fact that those of the younger generation of colonists, who are to-day loudly inveighing against any scheme of Imperial federation, are simply re-echoing the outworn traditions of Downing Street. In the admirable Autobiography[1] of the late Sir Henry Taylor—a work which every thoughtful colonist with literary proclivities should peruse—there will be found the text of an official minute to Mr. Fortescue, afterwards Lord Carlingford, and then Under-Secretary of State for the Colonies, which gives expression to the views at that time held *inside* the Colonial Office, in very plain and unmistakable terms. So far as the opinions are concerned, much of this document might have been the production of a member of the Australian Natives Association. I will quote a sentence or two:—

"The North American, like the Australian colonies, and like the Cape, have very naturally renounced all consideration of English interests, and renounced and resented every exercise of English power, so often as they conflicted, in the slightest degree, with colonial interests or sentiments. If (notwithstanding the Irish element in their populations) they have any *sentiment* of attachment to England (which I doubt), it is one which is ready to be converted into actual animosity on the slightest conflict of interests, or interference with inde-

---

[1] Vol. ii. pp. 237-8.

pendent action. So long as the connection is an unequal one—all *give* and no *take*—and they enjoy real independence, they are content; but no longer."

This was written as far back as March 25th, 1865. Twenty years afterwards the retired Downing Street official appended the following footnote to the very passage I have quoted :—"*Feb.* 1885.—In the very week in which this chapter is passing through the press, the Canadian and Australasian colonies have taken steps which are at direct variance with the views I have expressed, whether as to facts or as to forecasts. They have offered to contribute at their own cost contingents of colonial troops to our forces at war in the Soudan. It was not without reason that I concluded my letter to Mr. Merivale, with the acknowledgment that on political questions my opinions are nothing more than conjectures." In these words Sir Henry Taylor, with the gracious frankness so characteristic of him, admits that these recent events seem destructive of the theory which he had held and endeavoured to enforce on the colonial question for the best part of a lifetime. It was until very recently the traditional policy of the head permanent officials in the Colonial Office, and originated with the ablest of them, Sir James Stephen, whose abilities and personality were so great that he not only dominated all the Colonial Ministers of that time, except the late Earl of Derby, then Lord Stanley, but succeeded in training such high-class permanent officials as Sir Henry Taylor and Sir Frederic Rogers (Lord Blachford) to uphold and promote this policy of disintegration. About this time this was also the accepted policy of many of the leading Liberal politicians of the day, and the granting of self-government to remote dependencies was based on its expediency as an intermediate and necessary step in the direction of their complete independence. The sooner, they thought, this final severance with Great Britain took place the better, so long as the separation was effected in mutual amity.

Now it is an undeniable fact that these opinions were never held by any considerable section or by any political party in Australia.[1] In fact, with the solitary exception of Dr. Lang, no Australian public man of recognised position has ever formulated a scheme of Australian independence. In his case, too, it was simply regarded as an unaccountable eccentricity, although it would be very unjust to

[1] See Appendix B, Sir C. Gavan Duffy's " Royal Commission."

that self-willed, but singularly able and honest public man, to affirm that he had not given the subject much thought and attention. Of all his numerous political publications on the colonies, that entitled "The Coming Event, or Freedom and Independence for the Seven United Provinces of Australia," published in 1870, is the least like an elongated party pamphlet, and the nearest approach to a reasoned political treatise. This elaborate work Dr. Lang, in a glowing dedication, addressed "to the Electors of the City of Sydney,"—that city from which, fifteen years afterwards, the Australian Contingent sailed to the assistance of the mother country in the Soudan.

It must occur to any thoughtful mind that some explanation is necessary of the glaring failure to propagate this faith in the coming independence of these great self-governing colonies. Why, if Sir James Stephen's theory was correct, has there been such a lamentable reaction? Why do we find Liberal statesmen like the late Mr. Forster and Lord Rosebery deviating from the creed of their immediate predecessors, and vying with the Conservatives in their advocacy of a formless but patriotic policy of Imperial Confederation? To these questions, answers might perhaps be found, at least in some cases, in the mere political exigencies of the hour; but we should still want an explanation of the colonial rejection of all these well-meant projects in favour of colonial independence. On this point, too, the Native Australian will be ready enough with his answer. Such deplorable apathy, he will explain, arises from the fact that colonial politics have hitherto been in the hands of British-born colonists. Wait until he and his contemporaries are in their rightful place at the head of affairs, and we shall forthwith hear the new Declaration of Independence. Most of this, of course, is mere harmless bombast—sound without fury—signifying less than nothing.

At the same time, I frankly concede that the typical colonist is decidedly apathetic with regard to Imperial Federation. I am, of course, referring to Australia, but shall listen very respectfully if Mr. Edward Jenkins, or any other recognised authority, assures me that the case is different with regard to Canada. For my own part, I do not think that the mass of the electors in Australia, while undeniably loyal to the English Crown and connection, give a second thought to any scheme of Imperial confederation. And there are many reasons for this. Of all men in the world, colonists find it most profitable to mind their own business. Milton's sensible line might be the motto of every respectable and prosperous colonist—"To do that which before us lies in daily life is the prime wisdom." In a go-ahead colony there are no leisured classes—neither poets, philosophers, nor paupers. Hence, as soon as a political scheme is mooted that does not deal with an immediate pressing necessity, no one pays the slightest heed to it. This condition of things has its advantages, but also its drawbacks. As long as the political sea is smooth, the ship of State rides bravely, but should an unexpected squall arise, the crew may be taken at a disadvantage. In other words, the relation between England and her Colonies is one purely of haphazard; we do not steer,—we drift.

In his felicitous speech at the opening of the Colonial Conference in Downing Street, the Marquis of Salisbury showed himself cognisant of this prevailing condition of the colonial mind; and, consequently, the few remarks he made seemed to me more to the point than the volumes of well-meant eloquence that has been directed, for the most part, to deaf ears. In setting aside therefore all these generous "aspirations" in favour of a world-wide English-speaking Empire, his Lordship put the business of the Conference before the colonial delegates, largely as a matter of immediate self-interest. And he at once spoke to men whose ears were wide open. In the following sentences we have, I think, the very pith of Lord Salisbury's apposite and sensible address :—

"Supposing that the colonies were not part of the Empire, supposing the colonies were independent, do you think that they would be safe?" (At this query, the colonial delegates eagerly leaned forward, and one or two of them bespoke heightened attention by the Parliamentary, "Hear, hear!") "I know," pursued his Lordship, "that twenty or thirty years ago it was thought that they would be safe; that their distance from Europe would make them practically safe, and that their only risk was being embroiled in quarrels in which the mother country might have engaged. But matters have perhaps changed, and are changing. I am very far from suspecting or believing that the rulers of the great countries of Europe are likely to commit any act of violence upon distant territories; but what I cannot close my eyes to is, that the facilities for such action have enormously increased in recent years. The great increase in the naval power of the countries of Europe, the enormous increase in the means of communication, place the colonies practically so much nearer Europe. The improvements of modern science, and especially of telegraphic science, aid the concentration of force upon a single point. All these things have brought the distant lands which belong to the Empire in various parts of the world within the sphere of possible aggression. Do not so misinterpret my words as to imagine that I conceive any aggression likely or probable on the part of those who wield power in Europe; but the circumstances in which we live, and the tendencies of human nature, as we know it in all times of history, teach us that where there is liability to attack, and defencelessness, attack will come. The English colonies comprise some of the fairest and most desirable portions of the earth's surface. The desire for foreign and colonial possessions is increasing among the nations of Europe." (At this point his Lordship paused, and the Australian delegates, thinking evidently of the Germans in New Guinea, and the French in the New Hebrides, again ejaculated, "Hear, hear!")

"The power of concentrating military and naval force," continued the English Prime Minister, " is increasing under the influence of scientific progress. Put all these things together, and you will see that the colonies have a very real and genuine interest in the shield which their Imperial connection throws over them, and they have a ground for joining with us in making the defence of the Empire effective, a ground which is not purely sentimental, which does not rest merely upon their attachment to this country, but which is based on the most solid and reasonable foundations of self-interest and security."

This was a mode of reasoning which, though couched in the unaccustomed phraseology of courteous diplomacy, was at once appreciated by the colonial delegates. If Lord Salisbury's contention that the colonies are safer from foreign aggression by remaining portions of the Empire be sound, then the problem of Imperial Confederation is practically solved. It would be presumption on my part to remind his Lordship that America profited wondrously through being an independent and neutral country during that long and anxious period in which England contested first with the

French Republic, and then with Napoleon, for supremacy by sea and by land. Not only was an American Mercantile Marine created, but the internal resources of the country and its population were increased tenfold. We have, so far as I am aware, no trustworthy statistics to show what was the absolute emigration from these islands to the then newly created United States, but I imagine it must have been very much in excess of that of any period preceding the Declaration of Independence. And it would be emigration of a more valuable kind, commercially considered; for it would consist largely of the industrial middle-class seeking a safe refuge for themselves and their capital. It will be said that I am debating this question of the continuity of the relations between England and her colonies, on the very lowest ground—that of material self-interest. In doing so, I am simply following the lead of Lord Salisbury, who, while by no means ignoring sentiment, yet very wisely endeavoured to show the colonial delegates that it was to their *interest* to remain part and parcel of the Empire. I repeat, therefore, that if he can succeed in showing this, he has practically solved the Imperial problem.

As his Lordship very properly points out, it is the progress of scientific invention, and notably of telegraphic science, which differentiates the case of the English Colonies in America in the eighteenth century, from those that now exist there, and from those in Australia. Not only, as he points out, do steam and telegraphy render remote dependencies more open to concentrated attack, but they also bring them in a perfectly marvellous manner within the radius, as it were, of the Imperial Government, or, as I should prefer to say, within the family circle. No one but a colonist who has resided in a remote province of the Empire, before and after the laying down of the ocean cable, can realise the difference. In all essential respects the resident in Australia or New Zealand is as well informed of what transpires at Westminster as though he were a denizen of London itself. In some respects he is in a better position to judge of the actual changes and movements of the time, for he receives his news in a concentrated form, and without any of the "dreary drip of dilatory declamation." In a word, the diurnal cablegram has the effect of making the remote antipodean realise that he is a member of the European family. How different was the case with the original British colonies of North America I need not point out.

But while fully admitting that Science has thus performed the greatest of miracles in bringing those who are divided by a world's breadth of waters into daily communion, I am far from seeing my way to the acceptance of any scheme of legislative union between England and her colonies that has yet been formulated. To my mind all these plans start on a false hypothesis. Herbert Spencer, in his felicitous manner, illustrates the evils of what he calls over-legislation by the instance of a man who slips and falls on the pavement. The crowd, instead of letting him lie quiet, immediately jerk him up, and probably increase the injury he has already received. In the same way, we feel there is something unsatisfactory in the relation between England and the colonies, and so we urge all sorts of violent remedies without pausing to consider that they might fatally dislocate the body politic. Nearly all of these schemes, however, are variations of one central idea—the establishment of an "imperial" something-or-other in London. Some of our would-be reformers propose that the colonies should send, in the ratio of their population, representatives to the existing House of Commons. Others would have a certain number of colonial peers in the House of Lords; while still another party would create a brand-new Imperial Parliament, composed of representatives of all or certain specified parts of the Empire, relegating to the House of Commons merely the domestic affairs of this portion of the British Islands. It is astonishing what nation-builders and nation-destroyers we all are with a pen and ink and a sheet of paper. There are even Australians and New Zealanders—not many, I admit—who are fascinated with one or other of these so-called Imperial Federation schemes. Can they for a moment realise what it all means? Take the case of Australia, with a kindred population, contiguous territories, and interests in common : it has, so far, been found quite beyond the skill of their most influential statesmen to federate any two of the colonies. Almost ten years ago Sir Henry Parkes proposed to establish what he called an "Australian nation," merely by federating New South Wales, Victoria, and South Australia—thus simplifying the problem by entirely eliminating Queensland and Western Australia; but though the projector was a tried politician and a Prime

Minister, no one paid the slightest attention to him except a Roman Catholic priest in Dublin, who composed and sent out a highly patriotic national song, entitled "Advance! advance Australia!" Yet, as one can well imagine, Sir Henry Parkes was able to show his fellow-colonists many reasons why such a local federation should at once take place. He pointed out that there were now three parliaments, where, owing to the agency of the electric telegraph, one would be quite sufficient; and this is a point that goes straight home to the tax-payer when the M.P.s receive a yearly stipend. He asserted that instead of three separate costly Civil Services, one could be established, which, by providing really high prizes to exceptionally capable men, would attract the best-trained intellects both of Australia and the mother country; and at a saving of a quarter of a million of money. He grounded his reasons for this by no means violent change on the highest considerations of statecraft. Could these three colonies be welded into "one powerful British state," he argued, "there would be a noble field for statesmanship, if the statesman could be found to occupy it. Sufficient immunity from the petty details of administration would attach to the principal offices of state to afford opportunity for the exercise of constructive capacity, which is hardly possible under the daily harassment of the politico-municipal labours of a colonial minister in the present state of things." And then Sir Henry, after asserting, of course, that other people's ideas of federation were quite impracticable, but that "the union and consolidation of the three colonies to which this paper refers could be carried into effect within a year," winds up with this very pretty display of blue-fire: "The United Provinces would rise, as it were, in a summer day, to an equality with old historical nations, and the flag of the Southern Cross would soon be known in every port of the civilised world."

Sir Henry Parkes is admittedly the shrewdest of Australian politicians, the typical "old parliamentary hand" south of the Line. And yet as soon as he takes to constitution-mongering his vanity bubbles forth like a boy's. There we see him, the political Bottom the Weaver, with his new and moving drama in which he is to play all the principal *rôles*, and, as the Lion, will roar you "an 'twere any nightingale." It is perhaps from a sense of the innate and boundless vanity of politicians that the public are so apathetic as to their nostrums. The great mass of the people are not unmindful of the laborious, and often disinterested, services of these performers on the public stage, but they sometimes grow weary of all this mouthing and iteration, and pay but scant heed to the trumpetings forth about new pieces and new players. For they have a shrewd idea that the pieces would be after all very familiar, and though the chief performer might come out in fresh and gorgeous dresses for which *they* would have to pay, he would be only the same familiar, much abused, but after all popular old favourite.

Since then, I admit, a practical step has been taken in the direction of Australian federation, mainly at the instigation of Mr. James Service, when Premier of Victoria. This was the result, as all such movements are, of foreign pressure. It arose from a sense of the weakness of the disunited colonies to resent the intrusion of powerful European states in the waters of the South Pacific, and was notably fostered by the characteristically reckless policy of France, which presumed to occupy the New Hebrides, a group of islands whose neutrality had been ratified by treaty, and then claimed the right to fill her precious possessions with the thieves and cut-throats, the *récidivistes* of her cities and jails. But after all, this "foreign pressure" has not been continuous enough to weld the Australian colonies into a single dominion. A kind of loose *Bund* has been established between Victoria, Queensland, Tasmania, and the still inchoate Western Australia; the colonies of New South Wales, South Australia,[1] and New Zealand remaining aloof. There is what is called a Federal Council, which Sir Henry Parkes describes in the spirit of Brown, the tragedian, gazing with undisguised contempt upon Smith's *Hamlet*, as "a phantom that pops up now and again at Hobart." So far the history of Australia presents a series of disintegrations, and the only successful attempt in the opposite direction has been effected in New Zealand, where the original provincial governments have been supplanted by a centralised authority, not, however, without the active opposition of a most influential section of politicians. Mr. Edward Jenkins would, of course, point to the example of Canada; but, if I mistake not, that great Dominion

---

[1] We just learn, by the cable, that South Australia has tardily consented to enter the Federal Council.

has been created purely by what I must call continuous "foreign pressure," both external and internal.

We thus see how difficult are the steps necessary to federate two or three contiguous self-governing colonies. How, then, can we expect at a bound to federate the Empire? For my own part, I do not believe it is possible to create an Imperial Parliament in the true sense of the term—a great Council of the Empire sitting in London and controlling all imperial, as distinguished from local, legislation and administration. From my point of view, the enormous amount of "foreign pressure" necessary to produce so vital a change in the Constitution would be much more likely to disrupt the outlying members. People who talk lightly of the task do not seem to me to realise what would be the immediate effect of their panacea. Even Mr. Jenkins freely concedes that Imperial Federation is a misnomer without Imperial Free-trade, which would mean to such a colony as Victoria the immediate loss of about a million and three-quarters sterling in Customs Duties. Is it possible even to conceive the misery that would result, and the wholesale destruction of vested interests, by the substitution for this of its equivalent in direct taxation? As far as I can see, such purely practical considerations as these never occur to the members of the Imperial Federation League, but they are the only ones that are present to the minds of colonial working-men.

Can nothing then be done, it will be urged, in lieu of the hopeless policy of *drift*? Is it, in a word, unavoidable that the British in Canada, in South Africa, in Australia, and in New Zealand, must inevitably disown the British Crown and connection, and become a set of independent and disunited Republics? He would have been a bold man who would have predicted anything to the contrary ten or twenty years ago, but, strange as it may seem, the unseen forces that are at work in the shaping of peoples and nationalities may now be tending in an opposite direction. Lord Salisbury has told us the effect of modern scientific agencies in exposing outlying colonies to the attacks of powerful but no longer sufficiently remote enemies. This fact has the immediate effect of compelling us, as it were, to huddle closer together for mutual shelter. In other ways, thanks to the cable, it is something more than a mere post-prandial phrase that Australia is as much a part of the Empire as

Yorkshire. I think also there has been another potent agency at work to retard the formation of new English-speaking republics. Readers of that inimitable book, *The Bible in Spain,* may recall the dialogue that George Borrow relates as taking place between himself and the Alcalde of Corcuvion, that "mighty young Liberal," who, in the most backward and benighted province of Spain, held forth almost fifty years ago on "the grand Baintham."

"Excuse me, sir," said Borrow, "you speak of the grand somebody." *Alcalde.*—"The grand Baintham. He who has invented laws for all the world. I hope shortly to see them adopted in this unhappy country of ours." It then dawned on that most remarkable of English missionaries that the Spanish functionary was speaking of Jeremy Bentham, whom he went on to apostrophise as a "Solon! a Plato! a Lope de Vega!" The recorded scene is exquisite, but I refer to it now on account of the light it throws upon that great flood-tide of Liberalism, the aim of which was to renovate the world by subjugating its antique institutions, and which led the reformers of all countries to favour a system of republican equality. For a while this movement seemed to carry everything before it. South American republics were established, European monarchies were to be thrown down, and the Popedom finally extinguished. Then set in a powerful reaction. It is not possible now to trace this step by step, but some of the great central facts of recent history have burnt themselves into the consciousness of mankind. The American Civil War showed that the old Liberal theory, that war was a game at which kings played with the lives of their subjects, was no longer tenable. Republicans, it was seen, could shoot each other down in the most wholesale fashion on a mere question of State Rights. The South American colonies, after they had cut themselves adrift from Spain and Portugal, "those effete old sacerdotal nations," went on in much the same ignominious fashion as before. But, above all, France, which alone among the nations of Europe had entirely broken with her past, pursued, under republican institutions, the old traditional policy of bloodshed tempered by epigram; while, mainly owing to the instability of her institutions, the direful and direct result of the Revolution, she has been entirely overwhelmed by her hereditary foe, who, to complete the contrast, has been enabled to re-unite under a common Sovereign, through the genius of a despotic Minister.

It is this succession of mournful spectacles which has abated the enthusiasm of generous natures. Men no longer believe, like the Alcalde, that Jeremy Bentham, or any one else, could invent equitable laws capable of removing the ills of the world. The Republic of George Washington, or of Abraham Lincoln, undoubtedly cuts a great figure in history, but what of that of M. Grévy? Reflections such as these all unconsciously pass through the minds of the rising generation of Canadians, Australians, and New Zealanders, whenever they can find time to idly speculate on the future of their countries. And, as Matthew Arnold would have said, they " make for " Imperial unity. Here, then, we have, I venture to think, the *crux* of the entire problem. Can these great and growing colonies forthwith form something approaching to an *alliance* with England? Can they, in other words, as they increase in power and population, be received *on equal terms* into the Imperial *bund*? Nothing else, I am convinced, will permanently satisfy them.

This is a subject which, I think, can be very fairly reasoned out between Englishmen, Australians, and

Canadians to their mutual advantage. The only link now binding England to these great self-governing colonies, which may be described as a link of dependence, rather than one of fraternal alliance, is that of the Imperial officer, known as the Governor. Could not an immediate reform be instituted with regard to the method of his appointment? At present he is purely the nominee of the Secretary of State for the time being. Why should not the colonists, under the direct supervision of the Crown, have a voice in the selection of their chief official?

Would we keep together our world-wide Empire, we may learn something from that most venerable of human institutions, the Roman Church, which Hobbes so well described as "the ghost of the Roman Empire." Under the most absolute of bureaucratic despotisms, scope is yet permitted for what, in default of a better phrase, I must call "Home Rule." Particularly in modern times the Church has felt the danger of sending mere Italian nominees into distant provinces, a practice that more than anything else helped to destroy the prestige of the Pope in England, and to bring on the Reformation in both parts of this island. In the selection of a bishop, therefore, the diocese very properly has a voice, and the practice obtains of submitting the names of three eligible ecclesiastics to his Holiness, whose individual claims are further distinguished by the words *dignus, dignior, dignissimus*. Why could not this admirable plan be imitated in the matter of selecting a Governor for a self-governing colony? Under the present system, it is a mere matter of chance who is sent out, and the most politic thing for a Colonial Office nominee to do, whatever his individual capacity may be, is to transform himself into a gentlemanly cipher. Take the case of Victoria, which I do the more readily, because the present representative of her Majesty in that colony is admittedly an admirable Governor. Let us suppose Sir Henry Loch's term of office ended. During his *régime* events have moved quickly; a conference has been held in Downing Street, at which, for the first time, her Majesty's British Ministers have met her Majesty's Colonial Ministers on something like equal terms, to discuss matters affecting the whole Empire. This has very rightly been regarded as a distinct epoch in the relations between England and her colonies. But does it not make the selection of a Governor for any of the colonies, who were thus represented at the Council-table in Downing Street, a very invidious task for the Minister who may happen to be at the head of the Colonial Office? Would it not be much better if the colonies had an actual voice in the selection, and could submit to her Majesty, through the Imperial Prime Minister, three or more names from which the selection of a Governor might be made? Under this arrangement, without severing the Imperial tie, this supreme office would thus be open to the honourable ambition of a colonist. Let us imagine, as I have said, that a vacancy has occurred in the Governorship of Victoria, and that the two local Houses of Parliament meet in joint conclave[1] to suggest to Her Majesty the names of the most eligible men in the Empire for that post. It may be that the selection would fall thus :—

        1. Hon. George Higinbotham.
        2. The Earl of Carnarvon.
        3. Sir William Foster Stawell.

[1] The nominations of the joint Houses would, I think, be preferable to those of that " small Committee, generally of the Lower House, which has usurped the functions of the Executive, and which we call the Cabinet." Colonial readers who are familiar with Mr. David Syme's most original work, on *Representative Government in England*, will, I think, on this point, concur. Such a conclave, too, seems in every way better suited for the purpose than a *plebiscite*.

Or if the present Governor intimated that he would be willing to accept a nomination, it is not improbable that Sir Henry Loch, who has been so successful as a Colonial Office nominee, would on that account be selected to inaugurate the new *régime*. If so, what a vastly improved position he would occupy as the man actually chosen by the accredited representatives of the colony, over whose destiny he would preside, and not by the English official, whom so loyal a man as Mr. Higinbotham was on one occasion compelled to stigmatise as the "foreign nobleman."[1] Such a mode, too, of choosing a Governor would excite interest and attention in every part of the Empire, and the individual who attained to this supreme post would rank as a veritable colonial, perhaps Imperial, potentate, instead of being a mere highly-paid Downing Street official; and what an eligible set of Life Peers could be formed out of such a chosen body of ex-Governors, who would really be an acquisition to Lord Dunraven's reformed House of Lords. How, it may be asked, under an elective, or rather *selective*, Governor, would Victoria differ from an independent

[1] See Appendix C, "The Colonial Office and the Foreign Nobleman."

republic with an elective President? It seems to me, very materially, so long as the prevailing loyalty to the English Crown and connection exists. And so far as I see, there is no reason why it should not be permanent; no reason why the present tentative and unsatisfactory relation should not be transformed into a lasting alliance. In any case, the ultimate appointment would rest with the Sovereign, whose fiat should be final as to the *personnel* of her Representatives, and who, of course, need not be any of those suggested by the Colonial Parliamentary conclave. On his appointment, too, the new Governor, if a colonist, should come to Windsor Castle to receive his delegated authority from the Queen's hands. In other words, I propose to leave the final decision as to who shall represent Her Majesty in the great self-governing colonies to herself, advised, if necessary, by the local parliaments rather than that it should remain under the official patronage of the Secretary of State.[1] It seems to me that my proposal would help to in-

[1] However far-fetched this proposal may seem, it is worthy of note that Sir George Grey has for some time advocated a system of elective Governors for New Zealand. True, he has been scouted by the "practical politicians" of the hour; but on many questions it is still true that what Sir George thinks to-day, "young New Zealand" may act upon to-morrow.

crease, or rather restore, the prerogative of the Crown; and by putting the British Cabinet more nearly on a level with Colonial Cabinets, it would, I think, tend to bring about that grand Imperial alliance between Great Britain and her colonies, which can only be effected under a universally recognised and, on Imperial matters, actually dominant Sovereign.

Whatever the Imperial Federationists may think, this alliance will never be effected by centralising the whole of the legislative and administrative machinery of the Empire in London. London is undoubtedly the chief city and metropolis of the Empire, but, for that very reason, care should be taken that it does not unduly drain the outlying provinces of their necessary intellectual life. This is precisely what an Imperial Legislature would do. We should all be, I think, fairly satisfied with the tentative success of the Colonial Conference, presided over with such marked ability, by a trained official, who has nevertheless, it seems to me, failed to grasp its most palpable lesson. Such a collection of really representative colonial public men had never before assembled. The all-important question of mutual defence, upon which after all the existence of the Empire depends, was thoroughly threshed out in debate, and already the effect has been, on the whole, all that could be expected. It is hoped that this Council will be the forerunner of many, and that each of them will be a fresh link in binding us together. But why should such Councils be always held in London? Surely this scientific progress in steam and electricity, upon which Lord Salisbury very properly laid such stress, has its uses for public men as well as for the common people. Why, therefore, should it not be feasible that some future Council of the Empire should be held in Melbourne, Wellington, Ottawa, Cape Town, or Sydney? Englishmen must notice the excellent effect produced (even though subsequent "party" manœuvres wrecked his labours in America) by sending on a colonial mission a statesman of first-rate rank like Mr. Chamberlain. More than anything else it makes the colonists feel that they are of some account in the reckoning. It diverts, as it were, the public mind of the Empire to them, and they become for the time being the centre of attraction. This is exactly what is wanted as a check to the over-centralisation of London. Consider the effect of a Council held in Melbourne or

Wellington, attended by the Secretary of State for the colonies and one or two prominent English politicians! We should have daily bulletins in the London press as to the discussions of such a body; and by thus making, even for a few weeks, an antipodean city the political centre of gravity, we should, in my opinion, be welding together the scattered parts of the Empire far more effectually than by establishing what even the Prince of Wales regards as an Imperial Institute at South Kensington.

These suggestions are the rudest of hints, loosely thrown out by one who sincerely prays that there may be no fresh disruption among the English-speaking races of the world; but who, at the same time, has a feeling amounting to conviction that any of the new parliamentary panaceas, proposed under the name of Imperial Federation, would be the sure and speedy road to that deplorable catastrophe.

CHAPTER IX.

THE MORAL OF THE QUEENSLAND IMBROGLIO.

ALTHOUGH I have in the previous chapter dilated at such length on the general question of Colonial Governorships, the matter is of such supreme and pressing importance that I feel it essential to further discuss the recent dispute between Sir Thomas M'Ilwraith, the Prime Minister of Queensland, and the Colonial Office, on the subject of the appointment of Sir Henry Blake as Governor of that colony. In one sense I could not have wished for a better illustration of the utter break-down of the present system of nominating Governors at a time of any tension between the colony and the Colonial Office. So long as the political weather in both hemispheres is serene, colonists will readily enough pay the salary of the Secretary of State's nominee, especially if the latter boasts a high-sounding title. A political cynic would doubtless be able to extract entertainment from the spectacle of the "patriotic and Imperial-minded" Queensland Premier, who originally annexed New Guinea to the British Crown, thus wrangling with the Secretary of State on his right to nominate the highest Crown Official in the colony. But as Lord Randolph Churchill says, truly enough, we cannot govern mankind by " flouts and sneers."

The history of this Queensland imbroglio, briefly, I take to be this. Sir Thomas M'Ilwraith, despite his well-intentioned and historic effort to enlarge the Queen's dominions, found himself outdistanced as an " Imperialist" by his rival Sir Samuel Griffith, who was able to cut rather a prominent figure on behalf of his colony at the Colonial Conference in Downing Street. In revenge, Sir Thomas seems to have determined to poach on his rival's " Radical preserves " in the colony. Being a man of considerable force and individuality, with a party at his back, he had influence enough to upset the Naval Defence Bill which Sir Samuel Griffith introduced into the Queensland Parliament in fulfilment of his pledges to Lord Knutsford at the Colonial Conference. This was a very serious matter to begin with; and Queensland stands out, thanks to Sir Thomas, as the only Australian colony which has declined to ratify the agreement with the British Government for the maintenance of the local Australian fleet.

MORAL OF QUEENSLAND IMBROGLIO 235

Sir Thomas M'Ilwraith next proceeded to formulate what he was pleased to call "The Australian National Party," by which adroit move he seems to have "dished" the local Radicals, and won over that solid "Roman Catholic vote," which is usually at the bidding of the political leader, who fathers what is believed to be an anti-British policy. It is not necessary to enter into the details of the squabble between Sir Thomas M'Ilwraith and the late Governor, Sir Anthony Musgrave, concerning the release of a criminal, further than to point out how adroitly the former turned to account any possible cause of quarrel or misunderstanding with the Queen's representative. The next important step was the Queensland Premier demanding a kind of vetoing power on Sir Anthony Musgrave's successor. To this Lord Knutsford very properly declined to accede, but as if to show the fatuity of Imperial red-tape, he forthwith appointed as Governor of the important Colony of Queensland an official who was chiefly known as an ex-police officer in Ireland; while at the same time an Under-Secretary of State and an Earl was sent to New Zealand.

The English reader may at once discount all the

rubbish about "the general community of Queensland abominating the very idea" of having as Governor an "ex-administrator of coercion in Ireland." At the same time it is perfectly true, and should have been patent to the mind of Lord Knutsford, that such an appointment would be sure to arouse the more unruly spirits, and that to send Sir Henry Blake at a time of such tension to Queensland, was to play straight into the hands of such persons, and to redouble the popularity of the local Minister in his new but not altogether consistent or high-minded line of policy. We must, however, take human nature and the exigencies of party political warfare as we find them.

Let us, in any case, not descend to the easy but uninstructive practice of mere abuse. Better it were to employ that high faculty which Professor Tyndall terms the "scientific imagination," and bring it to bear upon Sir Thomas M'Ilwraith, with the view of discovering the actual conditions of political leadership in the self-governing colonies at the present day.

I would point out that the earlier political leaders —those indeed who have made Australia politically what she is—were of quite another type to those who have stepped into their places. Wentworth, Lowe, Higinbotham, and Grey were all men of old-world culture, for the most part English university men; but they have been succeeded by those who graduated in the rough-and-tumble of early colonial pioneer life. The old veterans, if their souls longed for an ideal condition of democratic equality in the new world, drew their inspiration from the time when they pondered, in some cloistered precinct, over the Republic of Plato; but, at the same plastic period of life, their successors had vexed themselves over the actual inequalities of fortune, whilst vainly "fossicking" for gold at the diggings, or trying to "run" a store on the very harassing system of "long credit" and "deferred payment." Many of the men who were to take the place of Wentworth and Lowe in the forum began their public career as local preachers and temperance lecturers—those modern representatives of the preaching friars of the Middle Ages,—who, like their forerunners, are almost always on the democratic "ticket," and against the established order of things in Church and State. From the pick of these itinerant preachers has been evolved a very considerable portion of the collective legislative wisdom of Australia.

Though lacking the old-world culture, and with far less comprehensive minds than their great predecessors, it cannot be denied by any impartial critic who has lived for a number of years in Australia, that many of these later and purely colonially-trained leaders have on occasion showed marked capacity for the guidance of public affairs in new communities; for which, I must confess that their serene ignorance of much of the lore and tradition of the "antique world" has often been, at least in the eyes of their less gifted fellow-colonists, rather a recommendation than a barrier. The former type of Colonial, or rather Anglo-colonial, statesmen, despite the occasional and not unwelcome intrusion on the public stage of a democratic "Fellow of Oriel," like Mr. Charles Henry Pearson, the present Minister of Education in Victoria, must be regarded as practically extinct. Whether the local universities will supply its place, the future alone can reveal. In the meantime, it has come to pass that Wentworth and Lowe have been succeeded, in the northern part of what was then the undivided colony of New South Wales, by leaders like Sir Samuel Griffith and Sir Thomas M'Ilwraith.

I have myself in Victoria lived through the transition from Mr. Higinbotham, who in my youth was the idol of the "fierce Democratic,"—to Sir Graham Berry, who, by his undoubted political instinct and great oratorical gifts succeeded to that giddy eminence during my later life in the colony. In New Zealand there is the same contrast to be observed between the veteran, Sir George Grey, and the younger and colonially-trained race of leaders, such as Sir Robert Stout, into whose hands the Government of the colony has naturally fallen. It is with this type—the colonially-trained, and more and more actually Native Australian politician—that British statesmen will be compelled to negotiate, unless both sides agree to part company without more ado.

Our present concernment is with Sir Thomas M'Ilwraith, the Premier of Queensland, and his dispute with the British Cabinet over the appointment of Sir Henry Blake.

In what I cannot but regard as a well-intentioned but very misleading article in the *Spectator* of Nov. 17, the subject is discussed under the heading of "Colonial Jealousies and the Government." The writer can only see—"In the 'indignation' which has been expressed by the Government of Queensland, the same political force which caused Mr. Bayard to dismiss Lord Sackville the other day so cavalierly, viz., the desire to conciliate the Irish vote."

But he does not ask himself the question whether it was wise or politic to furnish that "Irish vote" with a congenial field of operation. Further on he observes :—"The Crown not long ago sent a Home Ruler to Tasmania, and a very admirable Governor he was and is. What would the Irish party have said if the leaders of Parliamentary parties in Tasmania had expressed great 'indignation' at his selection because he happened to be a Home Ruler? Yet it is quite as great a breach of propriety for the leaders of Parliamentary parties in Queensland to express great indignation at the choice of Sir H. A. Blake on the ground—for no other ground has ever been suggested—that Sir H. A. Blake is *not* a Home Ruler."

This may be true, and yet not at all to the point. In every colony the Loyalists (who are, of course, the large majority), from their inherent character and nature, loyally accept those who are rightfully appointed to any office in the State. The Disloyalists, on the other hand, are by their very nature and character ever on the look-out for a cause of dissatisfaction and disturbance. Mr. Hogan, who aims to be an authority, tells the readers of the *Pall Mall Gazette* that "the Irishmen of Queensland loathe and execrate those heartless officials like Sir Henry Arthur Blake, who, in the prostituted names of law and order, were ever ready and willing to ride roughshod over peaceable citizens in public meeting assembled, and to ruthlessly demolish the cabins of the people at the bidding of insatiable cormorants of the Clanricarde type." We may smile at the "wild hysteric," but, in all seriousness, for Lord Knutsford to have nominated Sir Henry Blake to the Queensland Governorship at the present crisis seems to me one of those blunders which are said to be worse than crimes.

If his Lordship would be good enough to bear with me for a little while, I think I can make this perfectly clear. Mr. Hogan, who occasionally deviates into accuracy, tells the British public, with becoming pride, through the *Pall Mall Gazette*, that there are no less than "four Irish Celts in the M'Ilwraith Ministry." It is an uncommonly large percentage, though in most Colonial Cabinets it is found expedient to have one or two members in touch with the Roman Catholic vote. Let us try to picture Lord Salisbury endeavouring to govern with Messrs. Dillon, O'Brien, Biggar, and Healy in his Cabinet. I purposely exclude Mr. Parnell from any such combination, as I feel sure he would be too proud to join, save as its absolute Dictator. Let us further imagine Lord Salisbury, with these incongruous colleagues, suddenly confronted by the action of Lord Knutsford sending out to him as the Queen's representative an ex-Irish official. It is far from my intention to say anything rude or ungenerous of Sir Henry Blake, who has, I conceive, been placed in a very awkward position by his official superiors. I am quite ready to believe those who tell me from their personal knowledge that Sir Henry and Lady Blake would have made themselves most deservedly popular in Queensland; and that the loss rests entirely with the Queenslanders. But this does not at all obscure the issue that his nomination to the northern colony was under the circumstances an unfortunate one. Queensland, as we know, is in a state of unhealthy effervescence. Sir Thomas M'Ilwraith has "dished'

Sir Samuel Griffith mainly by annexing the local Irish vote. He is much in the position Mr. Gladstone would have been in but for Lord Hartington and the Liberal Unionists.

If it were thought desirable that Sir Henry Blake should become an Australian Governor, it would have been prudent, perhaps, to inaugurate his antipodean career by sending him to Tasmania, when Sir Robert Hamilton, who would surely have been a *persona grata* to the local Irishry, and who has proved himself, as the *Spectator* admits, a "very admirable Governor," might have been transferred to Queensland. Of course it is very easy to move other people's pieces on the chessboard, and, as I object altogether to the present system of appointing colonial governors, I should apologise to Lord Knutsford for unwittingly intruding upon his domain. My chief anxiety, while frankly admitting that I am compelled to form a lower estimate of Sir Thomas M'Ilwraith than I had before held, is to endeavour to be just, and to make the necessary allowance for the position in which he finds himself placed as a local Conservative Premier with a "Parnellite wing." Believe me, Sir Thomas is personally a shrewd, practical, business-like Scot, who gave evidence to the whole world, not so long ago, that he can feel the lofty inspiration of a genuine Imperial sentiment. It may be that the snub he received from Mr. Gladstone's Cabinet in reference to the annexation of New Guinea has converted a naturally self-willed man into a thorough-going pessimist, who has come to regard it as a matter of absolute indifference to his colony, who is in power, or what is the policy of Great Britain. For my part, I cannot bring myself to think so ill of him. I believe that he would be open even now to discuss on fair equal terms any real business-like proposal for consolidating the Empire. He has no real sympathy with lawlessness or with the rebellious spirit. He belongs by race and creed to the most loyal portion of the British nation; and whether his manner is agreeable or not, it is with colonial men such as he that British statesmen will have to deal, unless, like Lord Granville, so far back as 1870,[*] they think it better we should part company finally and for ever.

[1] See Appendix B, Sir C. Gavan Duffy's " Royal Commission."

I do not feel called upon to defend Sir Thomas M'Ilwraith, and I do not deny that during his recent course of procedure he must have appeared anything but a pleasant personage for an English gentleman like Lord Knutsford, trained under an utterly different social and political system, to deal with. We must, however, as I have said before, take political human nature and our system of government by faction, as we find them. These are, after all, much the same in London and in Brisbane. If Sir Thomas M'Ilwraith does not appear to us to cut a very lofty or consistent figure, what, if we really mean what we are always saying, are we to think of British statesmen in the first rank, like Mr. Gladstone and Sir William Harcourt, who have had all the advantages of old-world culture and the loftiest and most ennobling associations from their birth? Sir Thomas, it would appear, has "turned his back upon himself" for the sake of the "Irish vote," which means in his case a new lease of the coveted office of Premier of his colony. But I feel sure that he does not deceive himself or others into the belief that he is acting from any superlatively high or conscientious motives, like Mr. Gladstone, whose whole political career, despite his intellectual brilliancy, and marvellous vitality, can only be explained in the splendid phrase of Mr. Joseph Cowen, by his " Idolatry of the Immediate." Sir Thomas is a successful and vigorous colonist, of a rude and self-willed character. But he is, after all, of a manly type—springing from the yeomanry of Ayrshire, the birth-place of Robert Burns, and I am satisfied that he could never consciously "play to the gallery" without deep inward shame and self-mortification.

I have no doubt that the admirers of that distinguished ornament of the House of Commons, Sir William Vernon Harcourt, will be considerably outraged by any comparison between one of his royal lineage—the grandson, too, of an Archbishop —with his brilliant academical and legal attainments, and his cultivated capacity for persiflage, and a rude colonial Premier, angling for the support of a disloyal section of the community. From my point of view, any apology for the comparison is entirely due to Sir Thomas M'Ilwraith. As for Sir William Vernon Harcourt, his archiepiscopal descent no longer overawes me, for I have seriously come to regard his political existence as the strongest argument that can be adduced in favour of the enforced celibacy of the higher clergy, as in the Greek Church.

If Lord Knutsford has been sufficiently ruffled by the conduct of Sir Thomas M'Ilwraith to take a genuine interest in the *personnel* of Australian politicians, and is really eager for fresh information, I think he might devote a leisure hour to the perusal of a work of fiction, entitled *Policy and Passion*, by Mrs. Campbell Praed. In the character of Thomas Longleat of Kooralbyn, "Premier of Leichardt's-Land," he will find a striking picture of the self-made, aggressive type of colonial politician. It is, I should think, a study from life, for, as is well known, the gifted authoress is herself a daughter of Queensland. I do not say it is a very pleasant picture, and I think that in some respects the harder lines might have been softened, without any detriment to it as a portrait. But, as a character, Thomas Longleat is well worthy of study, for he is of a new-world type, with which our old-world statesmen and diplomatists may be more and more called upon to negotiate, on behalf of Her Majesty's subjects in Great Britain and the colonies.

Even when this storm about the Governorship has abated, it would be well if the Imperial Government would give some personal attention to Sir Thomas M'Ilwraith's National Party in Queensland. The following is its programme, as given in an admirable letter, dated Rockhampton, Sept. 9, 1888, which appeared in a recent number of the *Scotsman*:—

"(1) Cultivation of an Australian national spirit, with respect to all matters affecting education, labour, trade, and laws.

"(2) The federation of the dominion, with a provision for a system of Australian national defence.

"(3) The energetic vindication and protection of the civil and political liberties, rights, and obligations of the people, and the adoption of the principle that laws passed by the Australian Legislatures shall not require the imperial sanction to render them operative.

"(4) The fostering and protection of Australian industries.

"(5) The exclusion from Australia of the Chinese and other servile races, and the preservation of the entire continent as a home for white men.

"(6) The exclusion from the islands and waters of Australasia and the Western Pacific of all foreign convicts.

"(7) The active promotion of all legislative measures calculated—(a) to check the wasteful expenditure of the public money, to prevent the levying of oppressive taxation, and to guard against the abuse of political patronage; (b) to repress injurious monopolies, to allay sectional jealousies, and to prevent the creation of privileged classes; (c) to stimulate settlement upon the land and develop its mineral and other resources; (d) to carry on reproductive public works, to conserve the rainfall, improve natural water-courses, and tap the subterranean waters of the country; (e) to remedy all the abuses in the law, repeal all barbarous and obsolete Acts, and reduce the cost of law proceedings.

"(8) The return of members to the Legislative Assembly pledged to carry out the foregoing principles and objects."

With considerable shrewdness the writer observes that "on examining this programme carefully you will see there is a good deal of Home Rule about it, and that being so, Irishmen have adopted it with alacrity and unanimity." Here he places his finger on a very real danger indeed. In a short but suggestive letter to the *Times* (dated Nov. 19), Mr. Gowen Evans, who is so well and widely known in Australia, in connection with the *Melbourne Argus*, and who has only very recently come from Victoria on a visit to this country, observes:—" The Irish Home Rule Party in the colonies has taken *quite a new departure since the adhesion of Mr. Gladstone and his followers, and is actively employed in diverting the Australian Natives Association to objects quite foreign to its original purpose.*" This is very serious, and is full justification for vigilance, but not for panic. If only we are wise and prudent on both sides, there will follow the swift inevitable reaction of overwhelming loyalty, which will show the British people what the Australian public feeling on these questions really is.

The situation reminds me of an incident in the life of an Irish Colonial politician in Victoria, whom Sir C. Gavan Duffy may well remember, who, whistling before he was out of the wood, had the impudence from his place in Parliament to threaten a capable fellow-legislator by saying:—" I have only to raise my little finger and the honourable member will no longer sit in this House." This of course meant that the "Irish vote," which was supposed to be very strong in the victim's constituency, was to be cast against him *in globo*. But the nature of the un-

British threat aroused the attention of that large, but too often politically indifferent class, who, especially in democratic communities, are only too apt to exclaim, "A plague on both your Houses!" When the election came on, these quiet respectable men went to the unaccustomed polling-booths in such numbers that the threatened legislator was returned despite the "Irish vote," and the "little finger" that directed it, at the head of a most triumphant majority. This is the meaning for those who can see behind the scenes of colonial politics, of the division of fifty-nine against three votes,[1] by which the action of the Imperial Government was upheld in the matter of colonial Governor-ships, on the evening of November 29th, in the

[1] This Colonial Parliamentary incident is well worthy of remembrance. I give it in the all unadorned eloquence of the brief cablegram in which it appeared in the London press of Nov. 30th:—"COLONIAL GOVERNORSHIPS.—A Reuter's telegram, dated Melbourne, Nov.28, states :—' In to-day's sitting of the Legislative Assembly, Sir Bryan O'Loghlen moved that the House support the position taken up by the other colonies in regard to the question of the Imperial Government consulting the Colonial ministers before appointing Governors. A discussion ensued on the proposal, which was strongly condemned on all sides. On a division being taken at Sir Bryan O'Loghlen's demand, the motion was rejected by fifty-nine against three votes. The announcement of the figures was received with loud cheering. The members, rising to their feet in a body, sang the National Anthem, and gave cheers for the Queen.'"

popular Chamber of the most advanced and the most democratic of all the colonies, Victoria, when challenged by a local Irish Home Ruler.

This ought to re-assure weak hearts in a trying time. But for all that, I would earnestly reiterate my belief that a radical reform should take place in the system of appointing the Queen's Representative in our great and otherwise entirely self-governing Colonies.

APPENDIX A.

ROBERT LOWE ON THE DISABILITIES OF COLONISTS.

I REFRAINED from incorporating with my text this "note," with its eloquent extract from one of Lowe's finest colonial speeches, lest it should be urged that such diatribes are quite out of date since the inauguration of "responsible government" in Australia.

This, as I have endeavoured to show elsewhere, with regard to the appointment of Colonial Governors, is not altogether the case. But beyond this my book would be more imperfect than it is, without a reference to perhaps the most memorable and historic political gathering ever assembled in Australia. The occasion was a public banquet to William Charles Wentworth for his political services in being mainly instrumental in transforming what was originally a penal settlement into a partially self-governed colony. It took place in the hall of Sydney College on Monday, January 26, 1846, and some 250 really representative colonists, prominent among whom was Lowe, attended. The mere presence of two such intellectual giants, as Wentworth and Lowe, at the same festive board, in a remote dependency half a century ago, is of itself a remarkable fact. But my chief reason for transcribing from the columns of the *Atlas* (Saturday, January 31, 1846) these few sentences of Lowe's powerful oration, is that they are calculated to give the reader a more vivid conception of the "disabilities of colonists" than anything else with which I am acquainted. To the far-seeing mind of the truly Imperial statesman, for whom we are all waiting, this speech would, I fancy, reveal the secret of that deep discontent which we often find so strangely mingled with loyalty for the mother country among the ambitious dwellers in remote dependencies.

"Mr. Lowe, who then came forward and was received with rapturous applause, said:—He could conceive no higher privilege, he could seek for no more exalted position, than that of an independent citizen of Great Britain—possessing a voice in the Government under which he lived, fearing nothing from Queen or aristocracy; he stood in his strength, a part of that great constitution under which he lived, controlling his own destinies, guarding his own interests. To him the venerable fabric of the constitution was endeared by the consciousness of the freedom which it secured; his was the glorious past, the magnificent present, and the splendid future of his matchless country. Tyranny could not reach him, for he knew well that the proudest minister must quail before the voice of truth and justice. Such was the proud position of a citizen of Great Britain—such was the position he was entitled to under their glorious constitution.

"But if that citizen should see fit to change his place of abode—if he should have found it necessary to cast his lot in this land, governed as it was by the same Sovereign; peopled as it was by sons of the same race and of the same language, and entitled to the same privileges; then, indeed, was his political position entirely changed—then he lost the glorious attributes of freedom he once possessed, and stood a naked and disfranchised man, utterly defenceless beneath the lash of political oppression.

. . . . .

"The Imperial Government could declare war or peace without the consent of the colonies; although while the glory was allotted to the mother country, safe in her impregnable island fortress, the ravages and horrors of war were sure to fall upon her dependencies. On these great questions he would ask, if the colonies had a voice—a whisper, by which to make their claims heard. In such matters a ten-pound householder, in the meanest borough of England, had a more influential voice than all New South Wales.

. . . . .

"Deeply was the colony indebted to Mr. Wentworth, to offer their gratitude to whom they were assembled. He it was who gained for it the inestimable boon of trial by jury, and he it was, at last, who obtained the small remnant of legislative freedom which they at present possessed. Long and earnestly had he devoted his high talents and attainments, the great energies of his mind, to the welfare of his country. Amid persecutions and revilings he persevered, without hope or thought of recompence. In the face of power, in the face of tyranny, he took his stand, and he had not been able to learn that he had met with any reward, except the tribute which they were assembled to offer that evening. Rare and admirable men did, it is true, occasionally arise, who, despising alike the smiles and frowns of the great and powerful, devoted themselves to the good of their country and their kind—who, forgetting the selfish interest of the man in the feeling of the patriot, cast aside all other hopes in their devotion to their country, like this great son of Australia.

. . . . .

"*Many of his College contemporaries were called on*

to fill offices of trust and importance to the State. He did not feel envious of their lot; for he believed they would act conscientiously. They had been placed in those offices by the voices of the people, and when they acted unwisely they might be removed; but he, by coming out here, had not only closed to himself that path of ambition, but had ceased to be a part of the governing body—had lost all control over the political destinies of the community to which he belonged, and had sunk into the slave of those who were once his equals.

"If it were an offence to join his lot with that of the struggling colonists of Australia, he thought that political disfranchisement and degradation was too severe a punishment for it."

[This generous tribute by Lowe to the political genius of his only possible rival in New South Wales, Wentworth, was uttered, be it observed, some years before the latter had consummated his great services by founding the Sydney University (1850), and by establishing Responsible Government, under his Constitution Bill, which did not become law until 1856.]

APPENDIX B.

SIR C. GAVAN DUFFY'S "ROYAL COMMISSION."

THE years 1870-1872 were certainly critical in the relations between England and her colonies. The Imperial troops were withdrawn in 1870 from Australia. It was the year, as we have seen, of Dr. Lang's "Coming Event." Just afterwards Mr. (now Sir) C. Gavan Duffy was for a short time Prime Minister of Victoria. Lord Granville seems to have succeeded in convincing colonial public men that it was to their interest, as well as that of their particular colony, to promote disintegration. As Mr. Jenkins points out, even Sir Alexander Galt took the hint. Mr. Duffy seized the opportunity to move for the appointment of a Royal Commission, ostensibly to report on the federation of the Australian colonies. The Commissioners, however, deviated into the wider question of the relations between England and the colonies. On this they were divided, but the majority proposed to meet the difficulty, in which Australia would be placed in the event of

APPENDIX 259

England engaging in war, "by constituting under the sanction of the Imperial Parliament the Australian colonies *quasi*-Sovereign States, subject to Her Majesty, with power to make treaties with each other and with other states, and with power to concur in, or stand aloof from, England's quarrels as may to the colonies seem wise and expedient." It was a very pretty and characteristic document, and bore the impress of its authorship upon its face. Two of the Commissioners, if I rightly remember, refused to sign it, and the Report had no influence with Parliament or the country. Mr. Edward Jenkins may rest assured that the Australian people would never shuffle out of their responsibilities in this pitiful way. But, as he has quoted the text of Mr. Duffy's Royal Commissioners' Report ("The Colonial Question," by the author of *Gina's Baby*), I cannot do better than give his refutation of the arguments therein adduced.

"No stronger hint could be given to us at home to arrive at a rapid decision upon our future Imperial policy. When the disintegration of our Empire is recommended by a Royal Commission, it is time to consider whether Her Majesty is to be Queen only of Great Britain, or an Imperial Sovereign. The proposal of the Victorian statesmen is unpractical. Such a relation of independent 'sovereignties' could not be maintained in this age;

and we have seen, even in democratic America, how the attempt to assert State sovereignty against confederated power was stifled in blood. . . . Before such schemes are further elaborated, may not we and the Australian colonies judiciously consider what claims the Imperial Government, representing the British nation, has upon those provinces? Colonial Ministers, acting under the Crown, have from time to time constituted small patches of society, excised from our own community, the absolute owners of property held in all moral and political honesty in trust for the people and Government of these islands; for it was won and maintained by our adventure and sacrifice. A slip of an imperial pen has unreservedly transferred whole provinces to those casual communities; but this has been done with the implied trust that they should be held and used only in harmony with Imperial interests. No Minister or Government had the power to confer more. These territories from which we might have drawn Imperial revenues are now administered solely in the interests of the settlers. We exact from them no direct pecuniary profit. They have been the gift by which we meant to reward the enterprise of our adventurous sons. But they must not suppose that they have the right to divest them of the Imperial *dominium*."

Every honest colonist will agree with these

sentiments of the Anglo-Canadian *littérateur*, whom many Australians, as well as his fellow-colonists, would like to see once again in the House of Commons. I can only hope, however, he has since learned that he need not have taken the futile Report of that particular Royal Commission quite so seriously.

But we might, with mutual advantage all round, have some light thrown on those political machinations. Why should the British Government at that time have been so anxious to cast us off? The plot, as we know, miserably failed; but the experiment gave a renewal of publicity, and subsequently of office, to a colonial politician, thought to be "played out." This was Mr. Duffy, who after his lamentable failure as a Land Minister, and his quarrel with his great countryman O'Shanassy, was completely "at a discount" in Victoria. But having profited by his House of Commons experience, he seems to have detected the drift of the Colonial Secretary's new policy more quickly than the local Legislators. Though only a private member, he contrived to get himself appointed Chairman of that spacious "Royal Commission." Shortly afterwards came one of those curious turns of the political wheel, so common in young democracies, and during a brief "interregnum" caused by the rivalry of the more trusted and responsible leaders, Mr. Duffy, who also had thus brought himself into some prominence again, became Prime Minister. Whether on a hint from Downing Street, or seeing it was no use in the colonies, the proposals of his " Royal Commission " were incontinently dropped.

APPENDIX C.

THE COLONIAL OFFICE AND THE "FOREIGN NOBLEMEN."

Every Victorian is familiar with the phrases in which Mr. Higinbotham used to denounce the Colonial office, and its typical head, the "foreign nobleman." Yet, as I have said in the text, the strong patriotism and intense loyalty of the present Chief Justice of Victoria were never for a moment questioned. His quarrel was not with England, but with Downing Street and its system of interfering with the self-governing colonies by means of despatches to its nominee, the Governor. Many Australians will read with interest the following thorough-going denunciation by Mr. Jenkins of the system against which one of the greatest of their public men was wont to inveigh :—

"An office, presided over by a shifting partisan, however able, however honest, however industrious —actually conducted by a permanent staff, seldom, if ever, selected for any reputation or experience in colonial life—an office, to visit which, is, for a colonist, like reconnoitring an enemy—to negotiate with which is like a war parley, and to assault which needs almost a forlorn hope and a battery—is, spite of any brilliant abilities existing in it, incapable of discharging, with success, the infinitely varied, numerous, delicate, and detailed duties essential to its business. To every colony, each with its own wrongs, or rights, or difficulties, such an office is sure to appear unwise or tyrannical; because, in its very constitution, its aspect is, to them, *foreign*."

One feels that the writer of these words is in earnest. As a condemnation of the *system* they are, no doubt, thoroughly justifiable; and every day should show us the dangers we run in not radically reforming it.

Of course, most of the glaring evils of the Downing Street *régime* were removed by the establishment of responsible government in the colonies, though not by any means all of them. I feel sure others as well as Mr. Jenkins would like to see a companion sketch to his own of the "Colonial Office," from the pen of Lord Sherbrooke, who thus described the system as it existed when he was in Sydney:—

"Let us see what are the links in the chain. The Governor who knows little and cares less about the colony, whose interest is in every respect

APPENDIX

anti-colonial, whenever the interests of the colony and the Empire are supposed to clash, is responsible to the clerks of the Colonial Office, who care as little as he, and know even less about us than himself. The clerks are responsible to the Colonial Secretary, who equally unknowing and uncaring, is besides, for *our* special benefit, a first-rate debater, whose head is full of Corn Laws, and Factory Bills, and Repeal of the Union—whose mornings are spent, not in going through that twentieth part of the business allotted to him as Colonial Minister, which it is possible for the most laborious of human beings to accomplish—but in excogitating sound pummellings for Cobden, stinging invectives for O'Connell, and epigrammatic repartees for Lord John Russell. This functionary is, in his turn, responsible to an Assembly, chosen for a great number of reasons—for wealth, for family connections, for moderate opinions, for extreme opinions, for every conceivable reason except one—their knowledge of colonial affairs. This Assembly is, in its turn, responsible to the people of the United Kingdom, in whose ears the name of colony is an abomination."

One must frankly confess that the latter charge in this diatribe is not in any sense true now.

In another article in the *Atlas*, the same writer was even more incisive, winding up thus: " Is not the result such as might be naturally expected from such a system,—that the Secretary of State knows nothing about us, except as much cram as may be necessary to make a speech to an inattentive assembly a shade more ignorant than himself; that the Under-Secretary knows just enough of us to adopt some crude and impracticable theory like the one pound an acre scheme, or the civilisation of the aborigines, to which he adheres with the desperate tenacity of ignorance and presumption; and that the Clerk, our real Governor, who is utterly unknown and irresponsible—who will not be praised if we are governed well, or blamed if we are governed ill—should take it as easy as possible, and content himself with echoing back the despatches he receives, *sometimes enlivening the matter by an occasional abuse of the Governor for something perfectly right, just to show he has an opinion of his own.*"

The last stroke is simply delicious.

APPENDIX D.

RELIGION AND IRISH HOME RULE.

For the benefit of my Australian readers, who will be pardoned for taking a lively interest in the present Home Rule Controversy, on the satisfactory solution of which the future relations of "Australia and the Empire" depend, I have collected the following notes on "Religion and Irish Home Rule."

The Rev. Austin Powell, an English Roman Catholic Priest, of Birchley, Lancashire, thus frankly expresses himself in a letter to Sir George Errington, an English Roman Catholic Layman.—(*Weekly Register*, Nov. 24, 1888.)

"For myself I must rein in, in front of the ditch of roguery and robbery. I cannot imagine it lawful for a Catholic to render aid to a cause which appears indissolubly linked with the nefarious practices of the condemned conspiracies. Such are my convictions, and I am happy to say they are shared by many sincere Liberals, and, of course, by all good Catholics hereabouts."

To which Sir George Errington in the course of his equally outspoken reply observes :—

"I am now reluctantly forced to admit that a great English party, instead of purging Parnellite Home Rule and restoring it to the level of honest politics, has itself been dragged down and identified with the same revolutionary and criminal courses which originally drove me from the movement. With these conclusions staring me in the face, I should be wanting in frankness to you and in consistency to myself if I hesitated to say plainly that as I withdrew from the degraded Home Rule of 1880, so I have now to dissociate myself from this fresh and more dangerous degradation—more dangerous because, in addition to destroying the fairest prospects of local liberty and happiness for Ireland, it has lowered the honour of English public life, and even threatens the safety of the Empire."

Nor should loyal colonists overlook the political significance of the noble Charge of the eloquent Bishop of Derry and Raphoe (Dr. Alexander) to the clergy of his diocese.

"We shall have more and more of unison of spirit with all that is honest and true in this divided land; with the noble-hearted ministers of the Protestant Communities around us, who have borne witness in the face of England to loyalty and honesty ; *with the tens of thousands of our Roman*

APPENDIX 269

Catholic countrymen whose voices may be overborne for a while, but who are inwardly with us heart and soul."

All the world knows what these Irish Protestant ministers think of Mr. Gladstone's Irish Home Rule policy. Forgetting old political divisions and social animosities, 864 out of 990 Irish Nonconformist ministers signed the Unionist address to Lord Salisbury and Lord Hartington; and of the small minority who declined to sign it, "only eight did so because they were in sympathy with Mr. Gladstone." Surely never were figures so eloquent.

If Mr. Balfour is spared to serve this United Kingdom a little longer, we shall yet hear the voice of those "tens of thousands" of loyal and law-abiding Irish Roman Catholics to whom the Bishop of Derry feelingly alludes. Meanwhile it is pleasant to find an English priest using such wholesome language as Father Powell employs towards the leaders of illegality and rapine in Ireland.

But my Australian readers will naturally ask, What of the attitude of the head of that Church in England, himself an Englishman? I have regretfully stated what I believe it to be in my text. Allowance must be made for that "usual law of reaction" by which "converts" to an alien faith generally become extremists. Apart from this, Cardinal Manning seems to me to possess the qualities and defects of a born party leader. He has probably long since recognised that if his Church is to play the masterful part, which he and those who joined it with him forty years ago imagined, it is essential that its leaders should be in harmony with the Irish, who form so large a portion of their flocks in London, and the other great cities of England and Scotland, and who are naturally not of the better type eulogised by the Bishop of Derry.[1]

[1] It will, I feel sure, be news to most of my readers, British and Australian, that there are only, according to the "Catholic Directory," some 1,354,000 Roman Catholics in England and Wales; but it is even more astonishing to find that at least three quarters of a million are of Irish birth or parentage. Deducting the foreigners, it is fairly estimated that the English Roman Catholics do not exceed half-a-million. Moreover, this element seems steadily decreasing, or rather it does not keep pace with the natural increase in the general population. See that most suggestive article on "The Roman Catholics in England," in the *Quarterly Review* for January 1888, the authorship of which has been so much canvassed in religious and literary circles. The writer, who is evidently well-informed of what goes on "behind the scenes," makes the following severe strictures on the Roman Catholic Archbishop of Westminster:—"Above all, the policy of Cardinal Manning has been to advertise himself and his Communion, by continually keeping it before the public eye, and by posing in his own person as an English patriot and philanthropist, though simultaneously abetting the National party in Ireland, and assenting to, if not enjoining, that dead silence as to the crimes of the National League, which has been steadily observed by the Anglo-Roman Episcopate, whose flocks are composed mainly of Irish by birth or descent, and who are afraid of telling them unpalatable, however wholesome and necessary, truths"—(p. 51). It is highly honourable to the English Roman Catholics, numerically a minority in their own communion, even in their own land, who, under the circumstances, and nobly led by the Duke of Norfolk, have remained so faithful to the loftier traditions of their loyal forefathers.

APPENDIX E.

EDUCATION IN AUSTRALIA.

THE New South Wales Public Instruction Act of Sir Henry Parkes, which came into operation on May 1, 1880, attempted a compromise of the religious difficulty, by permitting the teachers to impart religious instruction, and by giving one hour of each school day to the clergymen of the various denominations. In one of his admirable, but perhaps too frequent, *addenda* to the *Cruise of the Bacchante*, the Rev. J. N. Dalton, who, as an English clergyman, may be surely taken as an impartial critic, remarks: "The Act was passed almost unanimously, both by the Upper and Lower Houses, and the feeling in the colony is intensely strong in favour of a religious instruction. It is provided that the *minimum* four hours a day of secular instruction to be given by the schoolmaster shall include general religious instruction free from special dogma. But to meet the views of denominationalists, for whom this general religious instruction is not enough, it is further provided that certified religious teachers shall have access to the public schools, and that one hour in five shall be available for the special religious instruction of the children belonging to the church of the visiting religious teacher. Common Christianity is thus taught by the schoolmaster; special dogmatic teaching is given by the clergyman. The Roman Catholics, however, object strongly to any secular instruction, even of the simplest kind, being given to their children except by Roman Catholic teachers."

Hence it is that Sir Henry Parkes' well-meant compromise has met with no more approval in that quarter than the frankly secular system of Victoria. It was recklessly denounced by the late Archbishop Vaughan as "godless." In the course of an admirable speech on the question, Sir Henry Parkes himself observed: "I cannot comprehend why Roman Catholic parents cannot send their children to our public schools. I cannot see, when we have of necessity to grow up together, to perform the same duties in society, to drive at the same ends in life—I cannot comprehend how it need interfere with the religious faith of the Roman Catholic child, when he attends school, to read, to sum up figures, to understand a little of the geographical features of the earth, with Protestant children—how that can unfit the child for receiving his religious faith. We must rub shoulders together, we must work in

APPENDIX

the same workshops together, we must follow the same plough, we must man the same ships together, we must use the same tools in erecting our houses together—and why should not our children sit side by side in being taught to read?"

It is surely evident that those who object to such a system of public education as this do so, not because it is "godless" or secular, but simply because they want the government to subsidise their particular church or sect, notwithstanding that "State aid to religion" has been abolished.

On the subject of the "Higher Education in Australia," I have received from Professor Herbert A. Strong, while these pages are going through the press, a further criticism, which, in view of his unique experience as a University Professor, both in England and Victoria, I do not feel justified in passing over in silence. Referring especially to the *curriculum* of the Melbourne University, Professor Strong points out: (1) that the anti-Darwinian biology is quite out of date in England; (2) that modern languages are taught in England, historically and philologically. Lectures are given in the literature of the subject by the best men that can be got. To keep pace with the old country there should be a Professor of Modern Languages conversant with the most recent German work in philology.

Further, Professor Strong thinks that each professor in Melbourne has far too many subjects—which is fatal to specialised efficiency. He then continues—comparing his present English with his recent Victorian experience: "The great point which I notice, as different here from there, is that the professors here are looked to in every case to take the lead in education. The clerks form an association to educate themselves; and at once come to us for aid. The Teachers' Guild have a professor (myself in this case) as their President. The secondary schools ask us to examine for them as a regular thing, and invite our co-operation in every way. School Boards again elect some of our number to co-operate with them."

Professor Strong winds up his communication with a very high eulogium on the *physique* and mental capacity of Australian students. He speaks with the greatest admiration of their enthusiasm and openheartedness. I quote these remarks from his letter with great pleasure, because his much wider experience and knowledge of the subject coincides exactly with my own impressions. Since I have been in England, it has in many ways come to my knowledge that the historic Universities of Oxford and Cambridge, and such institutions as the Science and Art Schools in connection with South Kensington, are doing much more for the general enlightenment and culture of the mass of the people than are any similar institutions in Australia. It is all very well to have a thorough system of State elementary education; but in these days we cannot stop there. If the Sydney and Melbourne Universities do not bestir themselves, I have no hesitation in saying, however offensive it may be to Australian vanity, that the Australian people, instead of being the best educated in the world, will share the distinction—with the Americans —of being the most generally half educated.

APPENDIX F.

"A TYPICAL AUSTRALIAN STATESMAN."

"LIKE so many successful colonists, Mr. Service is a North Briton, to which circumstance may be traced his sound practical education, his acute commercial instincts, his deep Liberal proclivities, and his utter absence of that too common weakness of the middle-class Englishman—snobbishness. This combination of strong qualities, and freedom from weak ones, has led to the establishment of the great intercolonial firm of "James Service & Co.," and to its chief having been twice Prime Minister of the colony of Victoria. Mr. Service's political career in Victoria has been a long and honourable one. It dates from the time when he acted as chairman to the Committee of the electors who returned Captain, now Major-General, Sir Andrew Clarke to the first Parliament of Victoria under responsible government. That was in 1856; and in 1857—more than thirty years ago

APPENDIX 277

—Mr. Service himself was returned for the then undivided constituency of Melbourne. . . . As Victorian Land Minister he left his impress on the colony, by introducing the first Land Bill, which contained the principle so dear to the Australian settler, of "free selection before survey." This liberal measure was thrown out by the local Upper House, in which body the squatters and their nominees were the predominant faction. Mr. Service promptly resigned, followed by his friend, the late Mr. Francis, a Victorian public man, whose name is still held in honour because of his bluff manly honesty and generosity, and, above all, his prompt refusal on two occasions of the dignity of knighthood. . . . Many years after this, Victorian politics resolved themselves into a sort of triangular duel between three men, all of whom were lately at the same time in England—Sir James M'Culloch, another prominent colonial Scotsman ; Mr., now Sir, Graham Berry, at present Agent-General, and Mr. Service. After the elections of 1883, the two latter decided to unite their forces and jointly rule the the colony, Mr. Service having the place of honour as Premier. The future historian of Victoria will recognise that Messrs. Service and Berry governed wisely and well. They reformed the most corruptly, or at least stupidly, managed branch of the public service, and, having left their house well in order, adventured with great daring into the untried regions of "foreign policy." From this date began the long unsettled dispute with France, with regard to the *récidivistes* and the Western Pacific islands. Then Mr. Service set himself the Herculean task of federating Australia, his bold and gallant attempt resulting in the Sydney Convention, and the establishment of the Federal Council. Here, say his admirers, we may see the germ of the future United States of Australasia, differing, however, they hasten to add, from the Great Republic of the West, by being in political union with the mother country.

"Under the strain of all these labours, Mr. Service's health gave way, and in 1885 he began his late prolonged European tour. It was in every way fortunate that he, the foremost advocate of Australian Federation, should have been in England when the recent Colonial Conference assembled in Downing Street, and that both himself and the Agent-General of Victoria were nominated as two of the Victorian delegates. . . . It is well known that Mr. Service impressed the Imperial Ministers and officials by his earnestness, practicality, and thorough mastery of the subjects discussed between the representatives of Britain and the colonies. It could not be otherwise. He was one of the most capable men at the Council-Table, and one who brought, as well as a hard-earned life-long experience of "provincial" public affairs, the instincts and enthusiasm of "Imperial Rome."

APPENDIX G.

THE HON. W. E. HEARN, M.L.C., LL.D.

INTELLIGENCE has just been received in London, through the Australian cable, of the death of Dr. William Edward Hearn, author of *The Aryan Household*. Dr. Hearn was born at Belturbet, Co. Cavan, in 1826, his father being the vicar of Killague in that county. The future professor received his early education at the Royal School of Enniskillen, and subsequently graduated at Trinity College, Dublin. His profound knowledge of law was acquired under Judge Longfield, then Professor of Feudal and English Law. On the opening of the Queen's Colleges in 1849 he was appointed Professor of Greek by the then Lord Lieutenant. It was not until 1854 that his connection with the colony of Victoria commenced. He was then chosen by a committee, of which the late Sir John Herschel was Chairman, to be Professor of History, Logic, and Political Economy in the University of Melbourne. Among his colleagues who formed the first pro-

APPENDIX 281

fessorial board of this ambitious colonial University were Mr. W. P. Wilson, the Senior Wrangler of 1847, and Mr. M. H. Irving, of Balliol College, Oxford, eldest son of the famous Edward Irving.

Professor Hearn's influence in the Melbourne University, and with the community at large, was from the first paramount. In 1873, on the institution of the Faculty of Law, he became Dean of that faculty, thereby resigning his professorship. By this means the bar that had previously prevented him from entering public life was removed, and he became a member of the Upper House, or Legislative Council. For some years he had been engaged on the gigantic task of codifying the English and colonial statutes. It is a remarkable proof of his all-round ability that when Professor Irving resigned the classical professorship, Dr. Hearn acted as *locum tenens* until the selection of a successor had been made in England, and it was said at the time that he was capable of filling every chair in the University. He is the author of the sound and admirable economic work entitled *Plutology; or the Theory of the Efforts to satisfy Human Wants*, and of a learned historical treatise on *The Government of England: its Structure and Development*. Dr. Hearn's masterpiece, however, is *The Aryan Household*, a work which places him on a level with the foremost thinkers of our age. All of these learned books, intended for scholars and students, were written and published in the colony of Victoria; but despite the disadvantage of remote "provincial" publication, they were at once recognised by competent critics in England as entitling the author to a place beside the late Sir Henry Maine. Dr. Hearn was a keen local politician, ranking himself with what is known as the "Constitutional" or Conservative party in Victoria. He was an apt and brilliant contributor to the local press. He was a member of the Anglican Church, and, after Sir William Foster Stawell, one of the most efficient among the prominent laymen who assist in the working of the vast diocese under the Bishop of Melbourne. Dr. Hearn in private life was a singularly genial man, with a rare fund of that quality, native Irish wit, of which we read so much in books, but see so little in actual life. His death will be felt as an irreparable loss both in the University and in the Legislature of Victoria, for it will be recognised on all hands that there is not the remotest possibility of adequately filling the place thus left vacant.

APPENDIX H.

THE LATE WILLIAM BEDE DALLEY.

This eminent Sydney public man, whose fame became world-wide by his "Disraelian *coup*," in sending the New South Wales contingent of 750 men to the assistance of Lord Wolseley in the Soudan, expired at his private residence, Manley Beach, Port Jackson, while this work was going through the press.

Mr. Dalley was a native of Sydney, and from an early age, by his oratorical gifts, his skill in forensic fence, and his dramatic ability as a *raconteur*, was hailed as a particularly bright specimen of native intellect and colonial culture. He was of Irish parentage, and through life a devout member of the Roman Catholic communion. Were I asked to name, from among the prominent Australian public men, those of Celtic-Irish extraction who have risen superior to what I have called Irish tribal or Sept feeling, and become genuine Australian leaders—I could perhaps name only Sir John

O'Shanassy of Victoria, and Sir James Martin and Mr. Dalley of New South Wales. From an Imperial standpoint, this is no light distinction; as the aims and aspirations of these eminent Australian Irishmen serve to justify those who believe in the eventual fusion and happy blending of the races.

For, let me point out that both Sir James Martin and Mr. Dalley were colonially trained and educated; they, from the first, rubbed shoulders with those of another creed and race during the plastic period of school-life.

With none of the literary taste and culture of Mr. Dalley, or of the legal acumen and judicial training of Sir James Martin, yet, in my opinion, Sir John O'Shanassy quite merits a place beside them. Perhaps naturally he had greater political capacity than either; but he had not the inestimable advantage of a "common" education with his British fellow-colonists. The result was that he was constantly reverting to the narrower plane of the mere local Irish Chieftain; in fact, towards the close of his career he had sunk permanently to that level. But, for all that, he had many of the great qualities of a true political leader, and the general community of Victoria, as well as his Irish Roman Catholic fellow-colonists, may well be proud of so loyal and stalwart a champion as he.

Mr. Dalley's career, unlike that of Dr. Hearn, has

been very fully chronicled in the London press; and very justly so. For though I differ from Mr. Froude in conceding to Dalley a foremost place among the small band of really great public men of the Antipodes, I cordially recognise that his career was a very brilliant and a very honourable one. I cannot, simply because of his dramatic way of exhibiting his undoubtedly genuine Imperial feeling, rank him with the "nation-builders" of our new world. But he was a bright and most accomplished man, with a real taste for literature and the fine arts; a faithful and loyal subject of our Sovereign Queen; and a true and loving son of Australia, where he was universally popular with all classes in the community.

Printed by T. and A. Constable, *Printers to Her Majesty,*
at the Edinburgh University Press.

www.ingramcontent.com/pod-product-compliance
Lightning Source LLC
Chambersburg PA
CBHW022056230426
43672CB00008B/1187